IRINA NAKHOVA

Zimmerli Art Museum | Rutgers

Rutgers University Press
New Brunswick, Camden, and Newark,
New Jersey, and London

IRINA NAKHOVA

MUSEUM ON THE EDGE

JANE A. SHARP and JULIA TULOVSKY

with contributions by

Gabriella A. Ferrari and Natalia Sidlina

This book accompanies the exhibition *Irina Nakhova: Museum on the Edge*, organized by the Zimmerli Art Museum at Rutgers, The State University of New Jersey.

Jane Voorhees Zimmerli Art Museum
Rutgers, The State University of New Jersey
71 Hamilton Street
New Brunswick, NJ 08901-1248
www.zimmerlimuseum.rutgers.edu

The exhibition is organized by Jane A. Sharp, PhD, Professor, Department of Art History, and Research Curator for Soviet Nonconformist Art, and Julia Tulovsky, PhD, Curator for Russian and Soviet Nonconformist Art at the Zimmerli Art Museum.

The exhibition and publication are made possible by the Avenir Foundation Endowment Fund and the Dodge Charitable Trust–Nancy Ruyle Dodge, Trustee.

Published by Rutgers University Press and the Zimmerli Art Museum

The Zimmerli's operations, exhibitions, and programs are funded in part by Rutgers, The State University of New Jersey, and income from the Avenir Foundation Endowment and the Andrew W. Mellon Foundation Endowment, among others. Additional support comes from the New Jersey State Council on the Arts and donors, members, and friends of the museum.

Library of Congress Control Number: 2019945195

ISBN 978-1-9788-1474-5

General Editors: Jane A. Sharp and Julia Tulovsky
Publication Manager: Stacy Smith
Copy Editor: Carolyn Vaughan
Proofreader: Carrie Wicks
Designer: Diane Jaroch

Photography credits: pp. 22, 70, and 71, courtesy pop/off/art gallery, Moscow; works from the collection of the artist (except *Skins*) and p. 75, courtesy of the artist; p. 24, Andrei Nikolskii; all other photography, including *Skins*, Peter Jacobs.

Typeset in Univers
Printed and bound by Puritan Capital
Front and back covers: Irina Nakhova, *Scaffolding*, 1984. Diptych, oil on canvas (plate 5).

Contents

Foreword

A somewhat disturbing new trend in the world of cultural institutions is the primacy of the "visitor experience" over the more educational approach that museums have taken over the centuries. We are encouraged to look at amusement parks and highly interactive gaming experiences as models for the museum of the twenty-first century and beyond. According to this notion, the visitor must be constantly overstimulated by the art, resulting in a state almost akin to the drug-induced comas of 1960s rock extravaganzas. Irina Nakhova's intent is quite the opposite. Along with her fellow Moscow conceptualist Ilya Kabakov, Nakhova creates conceptual art with a poignancy built from the collective memory of those Russians who lived and labored under the well-constructed myth of the Socialist agenda. Originally staging dioramas in her home in the 1980s and inviting the Moscow art community for a viewing, she made those spectators feel that they were in some sort of malevolent fun house rather than a Soviet apartment building. I think that her philosophical intent was to put the viewer "on the edge" and for it to be up to that person to decide which environment was real and which was an artistic contrivance . . . a dizzying dilemma, that! She rightly realizes that the museum must put viewers off-kilter in order to get their attention. The central work of the current exhibition at the Zimmerli Art Museum is *Battle of the Invalids*, an installation that was first realized in 2017 within the space of the pop/off/art gallery in Moscow's Winzavod art hub as part of the Parallel Program of the 7th Moscow International Biennale of Contemporary Art. Like a magisterial piece of cloth, this installation weaves together skeins of gaming culture, sports, and the fragmentation/destruction of the human body due to warfare. Past and present collide, East and West meld together, heartbreak and histrionics coexist, and while the visitor can take up the controls to move the players around the course, a fragmentary piece of sculpture stands over the game, to judge which side will be the winner. What a sumptuous array of layers in the story of art and history throughout the centuries. Fasten your seat belts and join the fray!

Thomas Sokolowski
Director

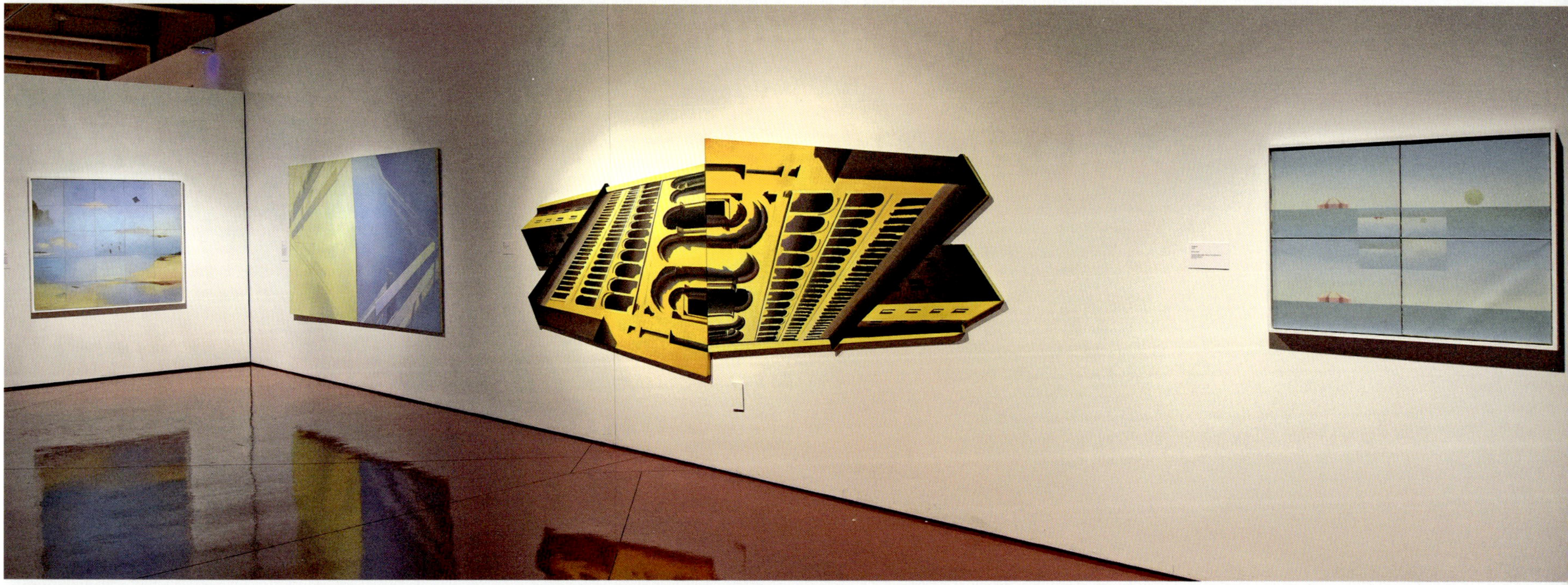

I've always been intrigued by the question of why society allows an unproductive, "parasitic" group such as artists ... to exist within its boundaries, and does not keep them in lunatic asylums, prisons, or poorhouses. Sometimes, it even gives them grants and otherwise supports them. Something is wrong here ... There has to be a reason. Art is the only thing that addresses freedom as such, outside of any restrictions. I think that society (probably unconsciously) experiments, allowing artists to work on the edge, while also granting them a "digestible" freedom which it can then utilize and expropriate.

IRINA NAKHOVA

JULIA TULOVSKY

Museum on the Edge

The exhibition *Irina Nakhova: Museum on the Edge* is the first museum retrospective in the United States of the artist Irina Nakhova (born 1955). Nakhova occupies a unique place in the history of Soviet nonconformist, Russian, and American art. She began working in the 1970s as one of the youngest members of the now well-known "school" of Moscow conceptualism. From 1983 to 1985, she created a different form of installation by transforming one of the rooms in her apartment into a "total" work of art, in whose realization the viewer, located within the space, was an active participant.[1] This genre later was employed by older members of the movement, most famously by Ilya Kabakov.[2] Nakhova played a prominent role in Moscow's unofficial art world and at times participated in performances and actions during the late 1970s and early 1980s. Since 1991, she has lived part of the time in the United States and has established herself in the West with multiple exhibitions and installations. At the same time, she maintains a residence and an art practice in Russia, which she represented in 2015 at the 56th Venice Biennale with the installation *The Green Pavilion*.[3]

Nakhova stands apart from both the older generation of Moscow conceptualists and her younger peers. Unlike many of her colleagues, in whose works the conceptual part was formed by a narrative component—text, story, or literary idea—Nakhova grounds the conceptual contents of her oeuvre in her dialogue with art history:

> *Art history references are very important for my work; I am constantly questioning my life, asking why I am here on this earth, putting everyday life in question. Usually I arrive at a mundane answer, "Because I can paint." But there remains a constant doubt in life itself, and this doubt also implies religious and moral questions beyond the everyday. I doubt art history the least, because I see, I believe, and I live by the greatest examples of art that set very high bars for me. Art history lives in a place of utmost peace. It sits there quietly, waiting for personal discoveries.*[4]

Nakhova's knowledge of art history and artworks in museums has consistently motivated her exploration of everyday reality. For Nakhova, the museum is a complex structure that is intended to last longer than individual life.[5] Museums preserve objects. Everything that becomes part of a museum's collection belongs to the future, representing the past. Nakhova's highly mediated and manipulated images challenge the limits of our own investment in the past. They cause the viewer to consider how essential the museums' artifacts were in their own time and what will be important to preserve in museums from our own reality, so heavily based on deception and disposability. In an era now dominated by "fake" news and ephemeral items, what will serve to form an image of us, and how might our current material obsessions represent our culture to the future? Nakhova also suggests that we should perceive the institution of the museum not with veneration but with a grain of salt, because it represents only a certain segment of the past, which may well be

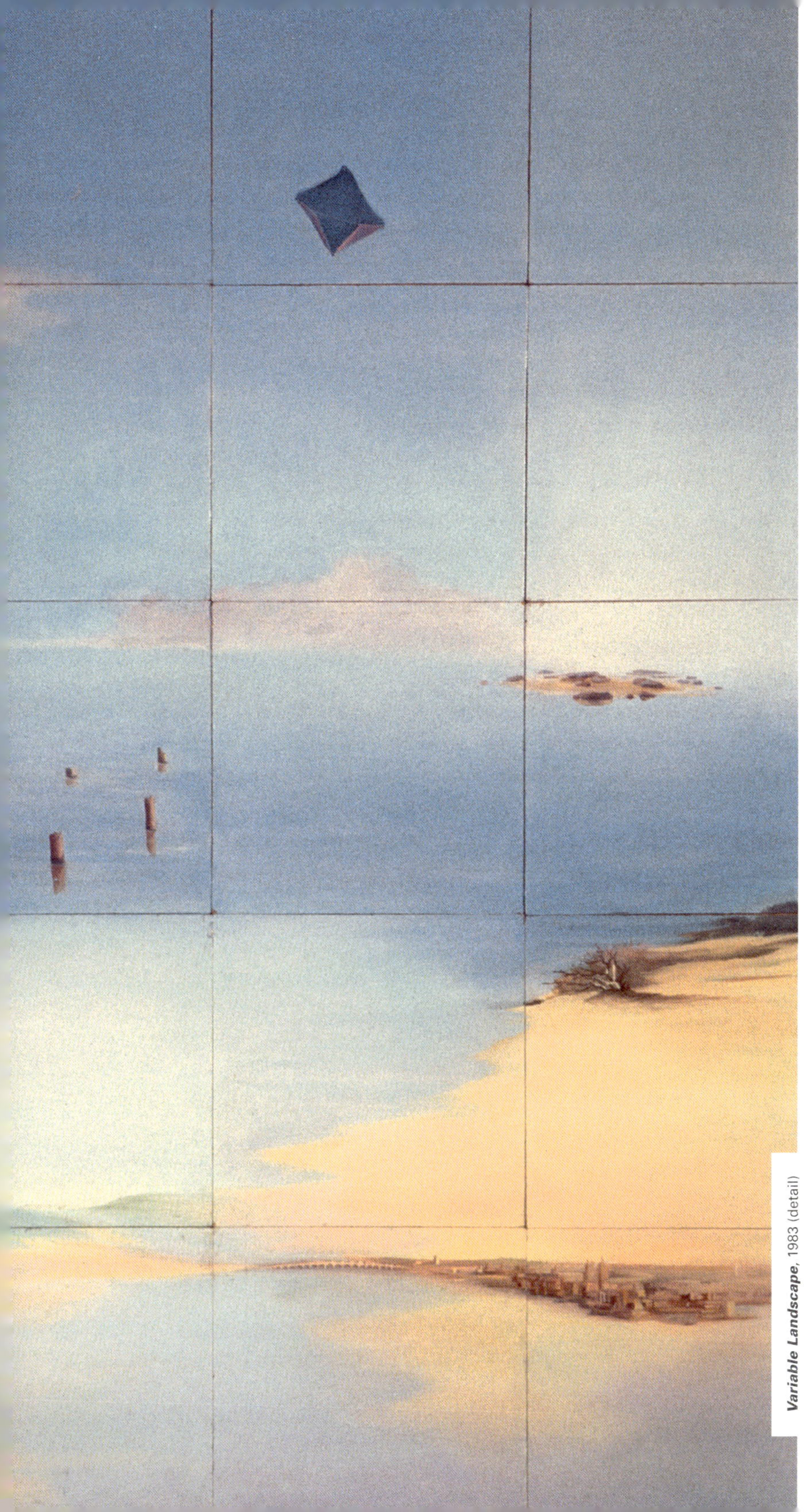

Variable Landscape**, 1983 (detail)**

a fiction. Nakhova's works therefore connect images from the past with materials grounded in the present to create a precarious projection into the future. Using the museum as a playground, the artist can challenge concepts of high and low, treasure and trash, revered and rejected, truth and fraud. The museum can be a place in which to think and to connect the dots between eras, a place of freedom for contemplation, a place on the edge of reality.

Museum spaces and the "space" of art history gave Nakhova an escape from a Soviet everyday life restricted by absurd rules. Later, after she closely experienced the West, Nakhova used the space of art history to escape from the absurdities of Western mass culture, yellow press, and false media reports. Nakhova often combines images from art history with mundane objects, forming unexpected connections and associations. By intruding into the lofty space of art history with these commonplace things, she transforms her works into surrealistic collages of meaning and concept, prompting the viewer to experience uncertainty and unpredictability of perception and interpretation both for the cultural references and for the work as a whole.

Nakhova formed this methodology of using multiple—multilayered—references in her early years as an artist in the Soviet Union. Many Soviet underground artists of the 1970s and 1980s, in their attempt to escape the restrained conditions of Soviet life, created parallel worlds that often manifested as layers of alternative spaces. This phenomenon can be seen in works by Erik Bulatov, Eduard Gorokhovsky, Oleg Vassiliev, Sergei Shablavin, Ivan Chuikov, and many others. Nakhova also learned this method of escapism to see through the image of the physical world into "other spaces." The explorations of various spaces—painterly, historical, or cultural—are intricately combined, and the viewer's perception of the mélange of meanings is the main concern of Nakhova's work.

This strategy of escaping into alternative spaces can be traced to Nakhova's early works from the late 1970s and early 1980s. In search of greater scope, she enlarged her canvases, creating an empty pictorial space where one could "travel," as seen in *Scaffolding* (1984, p. 12 and pl. 5). Minor architectural details, in this case scaffoldings, are present only to enhance the sensation of space. The same principle can be observed in *Variable Landscape* (1983, left and pl. 3), in which the viewer is invited to play with the order of the squares that form the landscape, creating his or her own version of pictorial space.

Nakhova soon complicated her works by adding several layers of painterly, historical, and cultural "spaces." In *Double Vision* (1988, p. 12 and pl. 8), she combines images from a book on the destruction of old Russian churches in the 1930s with an architectural landscape depicting ruins of antiquity. By superimposing these layers, she provokes questions about the signification of ruins, challenging the pastoral

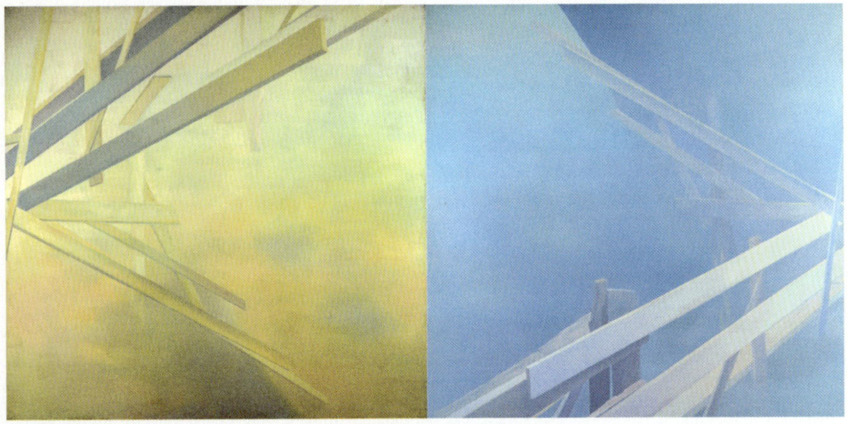

***Scaffolding*, 1984**

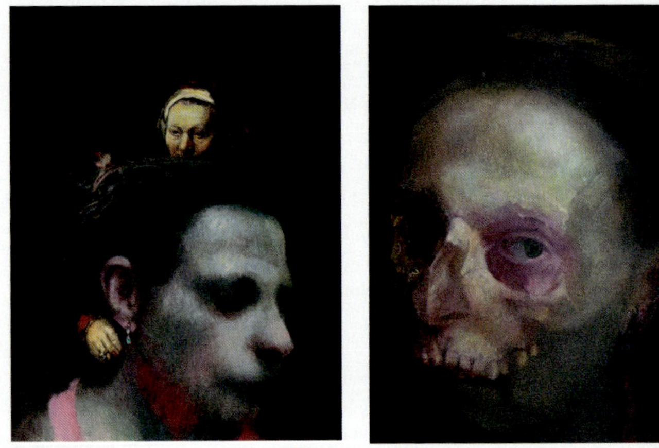

***Vanitas 1 and 2*, 2017**

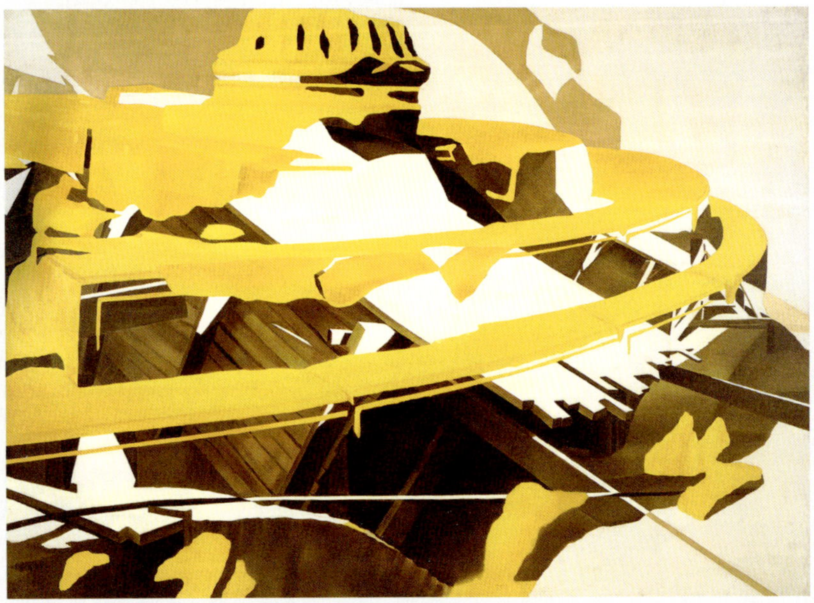

***Double Vision*, 1988 (one of four panels)**

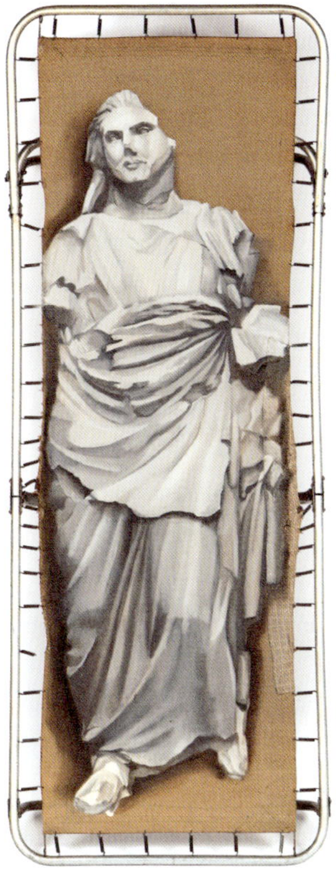

Camping, 1990 (one of a series)

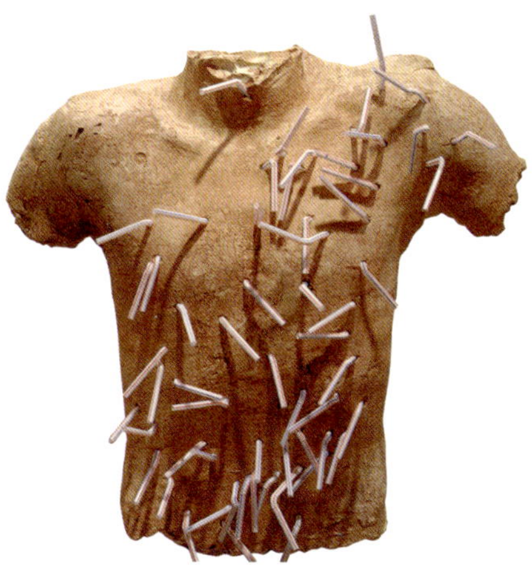

Four Torsos, 1992 (one of four)

perception of antiquity and reminding us that ruins are often the results of war or cataclysm. By adding such historical and conceptual elements to her paintings, she encourages the viewer to build new emotional and intellectual connections between the civilizations.

In her later paintings, such as the two-part work *Vanitas* (2017, p. 12 and pl. 30), Nakhova complicates the layered space even more, uniting the layers into an intricate fabric of meaning. Here the painting takes off from a photograph of the artist herself in a museum with Rembrandt's *Portrait of an Old Woman* in the background. The composition, facial expression, direction of gaze, and color prompt the questions of who in this work is real and who is depicted, who is dead and who is alive, who belongs to the past and who represents the present. *Vanitas*, the name for paintings that show the transience of life and the certainty of death, acquires in Nakhova's work a contemporary interpretation and an additional dimension pertaining specifically to art history and museums. She shows the fluidity of present-day life in contrast to the eternal but static matter in art, as if illustrating the adage *ars longa, vita brevis*. Nakhova also opens the way for multiple interconnected and often-ironic interpretations. By juxtaposing her own image as a museum visitor with Rembrandt's work, she, perhaps, contemplates her own place in the continuum of art history both as artist and as depicted model. The second part of the work makes those questions even more profound. It represents a self-portrait of the artist, her head now consisting partly of living flesh, partly of a naked skull, reality and pictorial fiction. *Vanitas* explicitly represents the theme of the museum and its time-connecting function.

Nakhova applies the same layered principle to her three-dimensional works. In the series *Camping* (1990, left and pl. 9), she combines old army cots with images of classical or medieval sculptures. An old cot is a not just a readymade but a unique object. It possesses its own history and individuality conferred by use. Nakhova, logically, places on the cot a person, in this case represented by an image of a statue, achieving a double effect: she humanizes the statue and elevates the cot to the status of ancient sculpture.

Multilayered space is also used in Nakhova's series of torsos from an installation at the Phyllis Kind Gallery in New York in 1992 (left and pl. 15). Nakhova made sculptures of generic human bodies with an allusion to antiquity. She then supplied them with absurd elements: plastic cocktail straws or indentations from heart-shaped paper plates. She made the torsos even more vulnerable by exposing their intestines or by embedding rusty cans containing kitschy figurines of angels. Are these figurines tongue-in-cheek allusions to the presence of a soul in the torsos or do they represent false spirituality? Nakhova's works, combining unrelated objects in unexpected but clever ways, always provoke ambiguous and multifaceted interpretations.

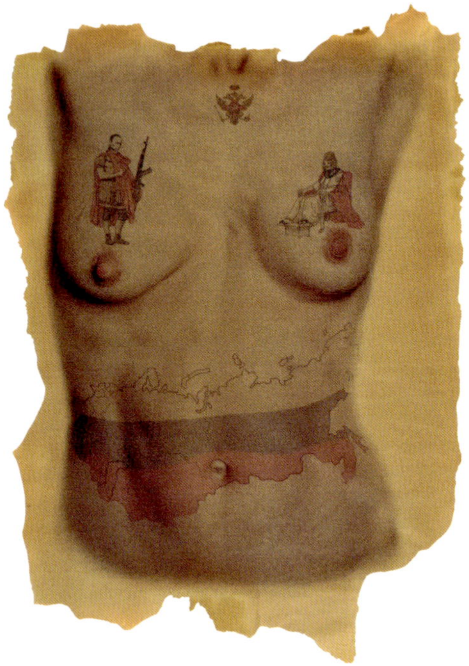

Skin No. 5, 2010
Nadezda came from a large family in a small town in central Russia. She wanted a different life for herself, and took a chance in the big city of Moscow. She didn't want to become a prostitute, and from her fellow girls living in Moscow's central train station, she learned that a prosperous gallery owner wanted to become a famous artist himself, and was hiring people for a thousand dollars only to be tattooed and videoed for his first art project. She was lucky to get the job. Unfortunately, later that day, she was slain by a homeless girl from Kazan. Rumour has it that the girl and a junkie from Lubertzi took Nadezda's money and ran to Crimea to spare themselves the cold Moscow winter. Her former friends near the train station amateurishly skinned her and sold her trimmings to an emerging artist for five hundred dollars. Her skin can be viewed at the artist's next exhibit at Access Gallery Foundation, by appointment only.

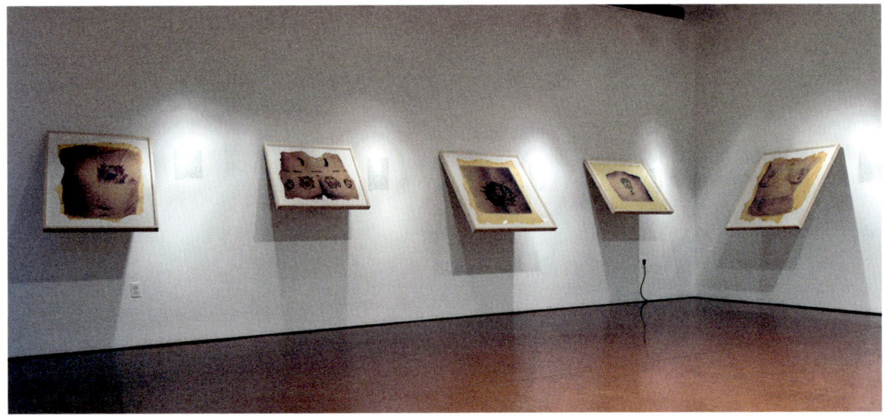

Skins, 2010, installation at Zimmerli Art Museum, 2019

The series *Skins* (2010, left and pls. 19–23) is probably the most provocative and controversial work in the exhibition. Each work represents a fake object based on a fake story. However, by placing it on display as an artifact in a museum, Nakhova validates it as an authentic witness of our current culture. Each of the *Skins* consists of an image of a tattooed human body printed on latex. An absurd fictional biography accompanies each one, explaining the relevance of the tattoos to the life of the owner. The texts claim that each of the *Skins* is preserved and placed on public display as an object of value. According to Nakhova:

Earlier, artists were dealing with fantasy worlds and bringing their spectators to something else, to different realities, expanding their worlds. Now, it looks like we need the opposite. You need to come back from this expanded reality to the reality that is right here. . . . It's needed in our world. We need to come back to the ground. We need to come back to our senses.[6]

Indeed, the screaming absurdity and pushed-to-the-edge kitsch of the *Skins* produces a sobering effect on the viewer.

The *Skins* also raise a number of controversial questions. What do these tattoos represent and why it is worth preserving them, especially by such a cruel method as removing a person's skin? Are they examples of contemporary folk art, tools of social identification, or unsuccessful charms against evil powers? What does this work say about our society if we must flay someone in order to preserve his or her memory? What has the function of the skin as a physical and cultural border between a human being and the world become? Was the poet and philosopher Paul Valéry correct when he stated, "That which is the most profound in the human being is the skin. . . . The marrow, the brain, all these things we require in order to feel, suffer, think . . . to be profound . . . are inventions of the skin"[7]

In her development of the museum theme, Nakhova works in a wide diapason from mass culture references to elevated contemplations of recognized masterpieces. For her series *Gaze* (2016–19, below and pls. 24–27) she took high-resolution images of famous paintings belonging to the Pushkin State Museum of Fine Arts in Moscow and then made video works in which she slowly guides the viewer through the painting by blurring the image and leaving only a tiny part of it in sharp focus. By doing so, she invites the viewer to gaze closely and enjoy the tiny details of the paintings. Nakhova studies differences in the way people perceive a work of art, producing several versions of "gaze" for each of the paintings. François Boucher's *Hercules and Omphal*e (1732–34), for example, is shown as perceived by an art student, a child, and an old woman. *Gaze* is also an escape, but into a micro space, which, as the work testifies, might be as dense and infinite as her architectural multilayered landscapes. For this exhibition, Nakhova created a video for the *Gaze* series based on a work from the collection of the Zimmerli Art Museum.

Nakhova's art not only pushes our notion of a museum to the edge but also broadens and deepens our understanding of the museum's value and its foremost cultural importance in a time when much of reality is virtual, disposable, or simply bogus.

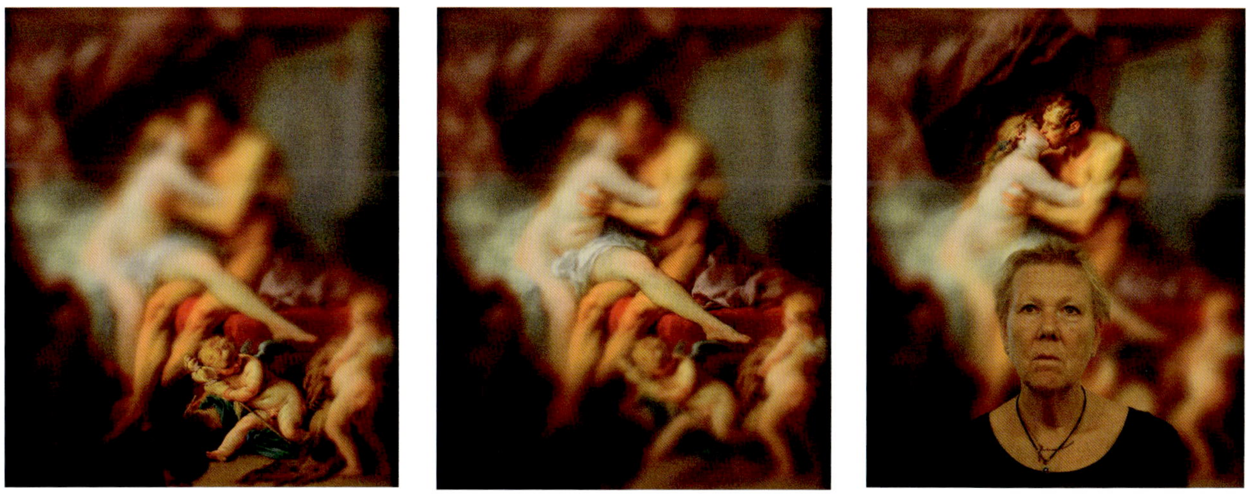

Gaze, 2016 (details), video, based on François Boucher, *Hercules and Omphale*, 1732–34

NOTES

The epigraph is from Irina Nakhova and Victor Agamov-Tupitsyn, "Detroit—New York," in *Irina Nakhova: The Green Pavilion—Russian Pavilion, 56th International Art Exhibition, Venice Biennale,* exh. cat., ed. Margarita Tupitsyn (Cologne: König; Moscow: Stella Art Foundation, 2015), 111–18.

1 See Irina Kulik, "Rooms," in *Irina Nakhova: Rooms,* exh. cat., Moscow Museum of Modern Art, ed. Nelly Podgorskaya (Moscow: Maier, 2011), 7–13.

2 Kulik, 7–13.

3 See note 1 for catalogue reference.

4 Nakhova quoted in Barbara Wally, "Impact and Refences of Religion and Art History in Recent Works by Irina Nakhova," *Rooms,* 57.

5 The following paragraph is based on the author's conversation with the artist on December 31, 2018.

6 Gabriella A. Ferrari, "First Comes the Feeling: A Dialogue with Irina Nakhova," in this volume, p. 24.

7 Paul Valéry quoted in Claudia Benthien, *Skin: On the Cultural Border Between Self and the World,* trans. Thomas Dunlap (New York: Columbia University Press, 2002), 7.

JANE A. SHARP

Irina Nakhova's Complexity: The Photograph and the Museum

Anyone who spends time with unofficial, or nonconforming, artists of the last Soviet generation hears a familiar historical refrain: that history itself was perceived in terms of a long, interminable past becoming future, with capricious and unexpected consequences for the individual in the present. The great writer and exile Andrei Sinyavsky (as the pseudonymous Abram Tertz) eloquently cast this perspective on history as an essential feature of socialist realism—the expressive mode of creative work in all arts that was enshrined in Soviet institutions and against which Irina Nakhova and her cohort defended their own.[1] Such a realization, a constant feature of daily life for artists, required a specific accounting of media, subjects, and audience, all of which are addressed in the interview and other texts included in this catalogue.

What emerges from repeated encounters with Nakhova's oeuvre is the viewer's awareness of the repository function of both museological and creative modes of work, condensed in the photograph. Although in the present exhibition Nakhova is not represented as a photographer in the narrowest sense, as a producer of exhibition products in the medium, photography underlies much of the work exhibited both as process and as layered imagery—it materially echoes in the sculpture, paintings, and even the cast figures for the interactive installation *Battle of the Invalids* (2017, pl. 28).[2]

The photograph was there at the beginning. Nakhova emphasizes the impact of viewing—more precisely, of discovering—photographs in the process of developing her own sense of identity as part of a family (she discovers the existence of a lost sister), and as an excised former member of a collective whole, whether it be school or the groups into which she found herself thrust while growing up in the Soviet 1960s and 1970s.[3] The photograph is as much a site of projection and inclusion as it is a demarcation of zones of exclusion—as the museum has been, over the course of its centuries-long history in the West. In the end, in all her various uses of photography, the image and the capacity of the medium to represent a factual, or indexical, present is contingent upon her purpose; its impact may be subversive or subliminal.[4]

Nakhova's diverse artworks reflect upon what photographs do: like museums, they collect historical narratives. This role is saturated with her personal recollections, too, of accidental and then surreptitious encounters with family histories and secrets. She reminds us that her father's photographs, which she discovered in his room, were primarily of Greece and Italy, places he had visited in his travels as a professional historian,[5] and she notes his neglect of people; few living humans populate the landscape or help her (or any viewer in the present) fix facts: the historical who, what, when of the photographic act. Yet these places had a material, cultural presence that Nakhova would apprehend as "real," not only imagined, as part of her own lived experience; they informed her immediate worldview and her creative persona.

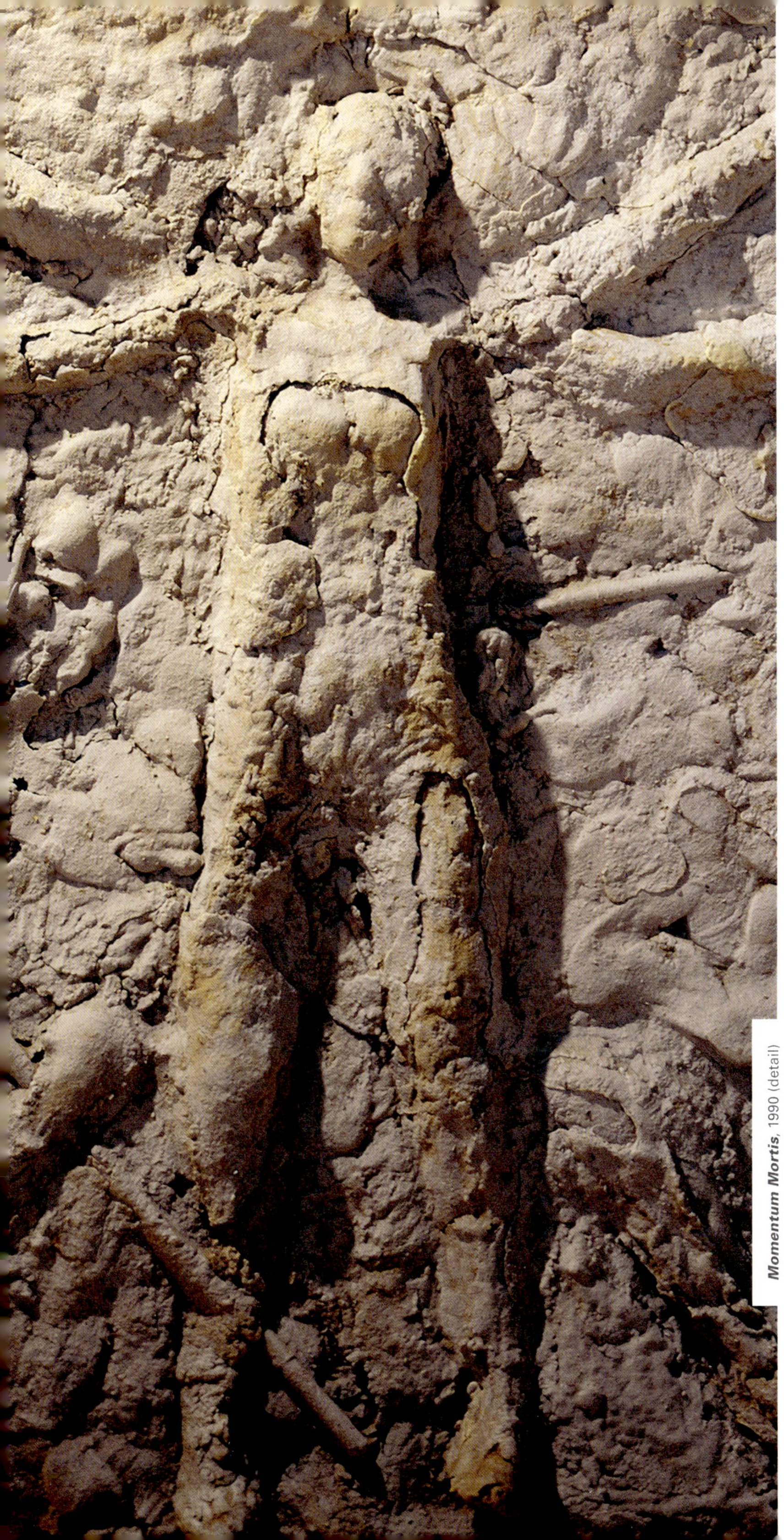

Momentum Mortis, 1990 (detail)

The resonance of those photographs, especially those of Greco-Roman classical statuary, shapes the choices made and materialized here, in the clay, earthen traces of the figures of *Momentum Mortis* (1990, left, p. 18, and pl. 11), the figures on cots in *Camping* (1990, pl. 9), and the paintings of numerous ruins—many too fragmentary to read as a specific architectural or spatial location (pls. 8, 9, 12, and 13). The ambiguous historical moment captured by the photographic trace poses the question: Are we reflecting on a common cultural heritage in the past, whether it be Japan or Rome, or are we immersed in our own memories of a personalized past now shaping our present? What we find, at least upon a first scan, are spatial, sometimes figural, abstractions. Fragments of buildings and perspectives coalesce and disintegrate as we move from object to object and image to image. The museum space itself revisits the ambiguity of the photographs underlying the works, propelling the passage from origin and source to material artifact, echoing the passage from past to present that their narrative elements disclose.

In this exhibition, as elsewhere, Nakhova puts into play the reciprocity of artwork and its container—the museum—as a destabilizing force that motivates and is generated from her aesthetic choices. The spatial configuration of the exhibition hall encourages both viewer and artist to exert consciousness of passage. We become engaged in an act of wonder, which, paradoxically, opens to critical reflection upon the cultural histories configured in the artwork. Such was the role imputed to the first documentary photographs and films in the Soviet 1920s, one that was quickly overridden by the need for a stable narrative (in the process of becoming) to be reaffirmed as material fact. The photograph would also be seen as a form of insurance, the guarantor of a future anticipated as fact (the utopian condition of the future perfect). This is not to say that Nakhova's use of photography directly identifies her with the historical avant-garde, with an Alexander Rodchenko or Gustav Klucis, at least not in terms of received accounts of their intentions (recent scholarship may undermine this past accounting).[6] But even their most "documentary" photographs present us with an unresolved riddle of the kind we encounter here: a riddle that is presented as materially real, before it slips away into speculation in the receptive moment of shooting, viewing, or recollecting.

Despite the frequent layering of photographic imagery in her work, Nakhova repeatedly underscores the distinctive role of painting in her creative world. The process of applying a painterly medium on a canvas is experienced differently from that of working with photographs, digital media, or sculpture. In her interview with Gabriella Ferrari in this volume, she characterizes her returns to painting as to a space of "freedom."[7] Yet perhaps even this sense of freedom is matched by the troubling ambiguity of the viewer's position in the presence of the historical photograph. There is something liberating, and unnerving, in the indeterminacy of the spatial coordinates of even her earliest paintings.

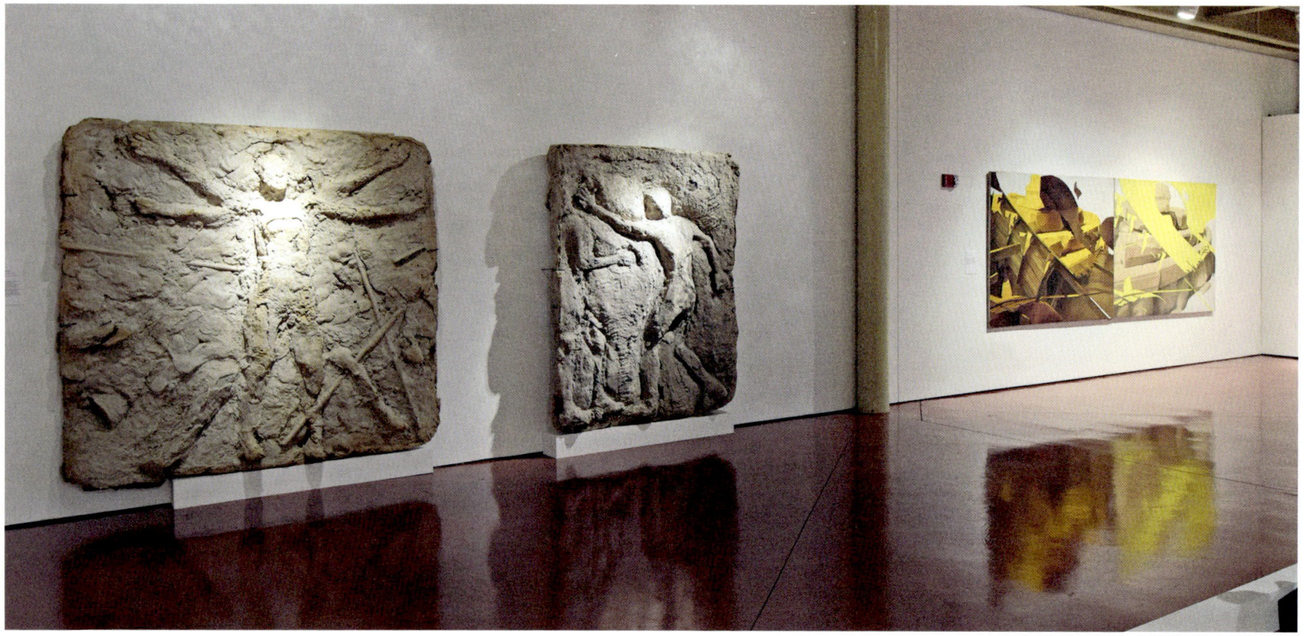

Momentum Mortis installation at Zimmerli Art Museum, 2019

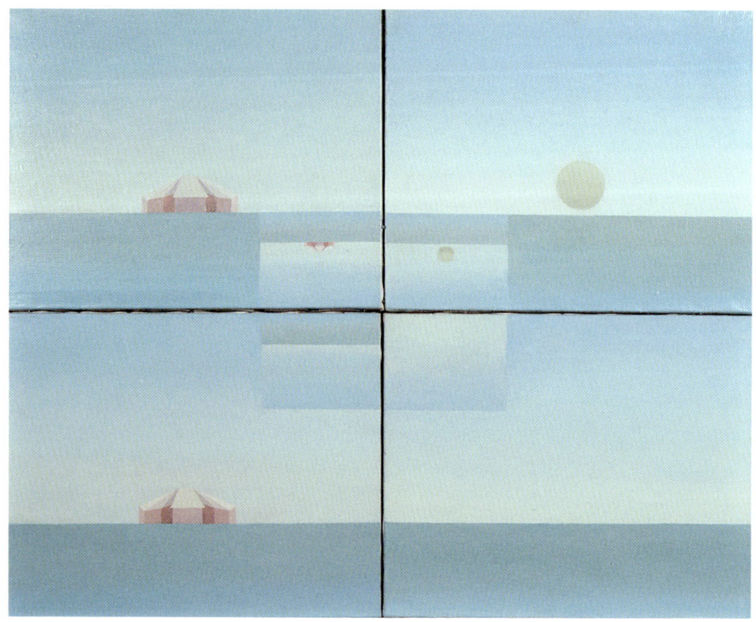

Untitled, 1978

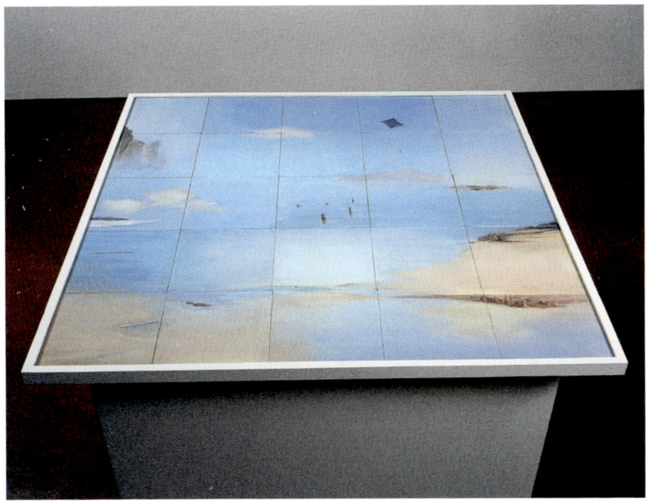

Variable Landscape, 1983

Quite unexpectedly, we may find the photograph's temporal ambivalence echoed in the structure of space in Nakhova's painted images. This is often achieved by a flipping of visual form derived from the spatial and material logic of the photograph: forms are inverted, shifted, and repeated along a vertical axis (see, for example, *Mobeus*, pl. 10). In *Untitled* (1978, p. 18 and pl. 1) and *Scaffolding* (1984, pl. 5), she deploys serial duplication to undermine our sense of the coherence of pictorial space; in *Variable Landscape* (1983, left and pl. 3), the viewer is presented with seemingly infinite possibilities of viewing points (starting with the possibility of reading the image from vantage points both "up" and "down"), because the work is meant to be disassembled and reassembled by the viewer.

We thus confront through our actions the power we should exert or explore when in the presence of the visual work of art. Yet the work itself escapes singular definition—by itself, it has no absolute claim on us or on a particular ideology (in a museum or gallery it may be mis- or re-appropriated). And yet it is only through the work of art, this particular work we encounter, that we sense our ethical freedom and obligation. This feature of Nakhova's work may be gleaned from even the earliest images we have by her; it may explain why she expresses a constant ambivalence in responding to questions of her adherence to and even opinions about, say,"feminism."

The way in which these works are activated in the museum underscores the open qualities proposed by the underlying photographs and peculiar spatial configurations of Nakhova's paintings. They are given specificity through location and time: the Norton and Nancy Dodge Collection wing in the Zimmerli Art Museum (a teaching museum at Rutgers University). Her retrospective is a post-Soviet event, and it extends its reason for being in the world to audiences and places beyond New Brunswick. If her work, in the mode of the photograph, remains a historical riddle—the museum, by "containing" it, shares in that precarity.[8]

NOTES

1 Abram Tertz, *On Socialist Realism*, introduction by Czeslaw Milosz, trans. George Dennis (New York: Pantheon Books, 1960). Many writers amplify these observations with reference to recent historical events; for example, Susan Buck-Morss, *Dreamworld and Catastrophe* (Cambridge, MA: MIT Press, 2002); Aleksei Yurchak, *Everything Was Forever, Until It Was No More: The Last Soviet Generation* (Princeton: Princeton University Press, 2005).

2 Nakhova arrived at the final form for this installation in papier-mâché by photographing statues at the Metropolitan Museum of Art in New York City, then creating a series of plaster casts and molds. The original conception of the work was sparked by memories of invalids—Soviet-era Afghanistan war veterans —begging on the Moscow subway. A detailed description was given in an interview with Irina Nakhova by Olga Danilkina, September 28, 2017, courtesy of the pop/off/art gallery, Moscow; see also Natalia Sidlina's discussion of the project in this volume (pp. 20–23).

3 Irina Nakhova, "Orphan [Sirota]," unpublished manuscript, March 3, 2018.

4 For an extensive discussion of Nakhova's use of photography, see Kalliopi Minioudaki, "Out of Extreme Necessity," in *Irina Nakhova: Rooms*, exh. cat., ed. Nelly Podgorskaya (Moscow: Moscow Museum of Modern Art, 2011), 43–55.

5 Irina Nakhova, "Two Halves of a Rotten Apple, or, Techniques for Separating the Body from Consciousness," in *Irina Nakhova: The Green Pavilion, 56th International Art Exhibition, Venice Biennale*, exh. cat., ed. Margarita Tupitsyn (Cologne: König; Moscow: Stella Art Foundation, 2015), 129–31.

6 See for example Erika Wolf, "The Visual Economy of Forced Labor: Alexander Rodchenko and the White Sea-Baltic Canal," in *Picturing Russia: Explorations in Visual Culture*, Joan Neuberger and Valerie Kivelson, eds. (New Haven and London: Yale University Press, 2008), 168–74; and Aglaya Glebova, "Elements of Photography, Avant-Garde Aesthetics and the Reforging of Nature," *Representations* 142, no. 1 (Spring 2018): 56–90.

7 A description of the viewer's role in interpreting the image and the link between empowerment and confusion may be found also in "Interview: Barbara Wally in Conversation with Irina Nakhova," in *Irina Nakhova: Works, 1973–2004*, exh. cat. Barbara Wally and Leonid Bazhanov, eds., (Moscow: National Centre for Contemporary Arts; Salzburg: International Summer Academy of Fine Arts, 2004), 13–14.

8 Interview with Barbara Wally, 15.

NATALIA SIDLINA

Irina Nakhova's *Battle of the Invalids*

Working on the reconstruction of Irina Nakhova's *Room No. 2* at the Tate Modern in London[1] has given me greater insight into the importance that direct engagement with the audience has had for the artist's creative practice from its very beginning. Nakhova and Ilya Kabakov were the first Moscow conceptualists to experiment with environments in the 1980s. Her series of installations known as *Rooms* (1983–87) provided an immersive environment that subtly addressed social issues and served as a much-needed platform for interaction among liberal-minded, creative people.[2] Working with environments and site-specific installations and projects continues to be at the center of Nakhova's work.

Nakhova's most complex engagement with site-specific projects to date occurred during her work for the Russian Pavilion at the 56th Venice Biennale in 2015. Her project, *The Green Pavilion*, brought together diverse facets of her creative exploration: immersive environments and engagement with the themes of memory and art history as well as commentary on political and social transformation. While the 1980s *Rooms* served as a stage for debates between key figures of Moscow conceptualism such as Kabakov, Andrei Monastyrski, and Joseph Backstein (the video recording of the conversations in *Room No. 2* in 1984 was featured at the Pavilion),[3] the 2015 project served as grounds for a spontaneous "occupation" by protesters against Russia's involvement in Ukraine.[4]

Nakhova recounted that she found her initial inspiration for *Battle of the Invalids* while developing *The Green Pavilion*:

I had so many ideas during my work on the pavilion; only three made it to the final cut and only one was realized as The Green Pavilion. . . . [I recalled] a group of invalids without legs who were active in the Oktyabrskaya metro station. Apparently, they were [soldiers] disabled during the war in Afghanistan. They would ride through the carriages, begging. I was shocked, on the one hand, by their carts made out of wooden boxes, with dreadful wheels, by the horror and senselessness and, on the other, by the irony—beggars are usually controlled by the Mafia. This image haunted me.[5]

The project was first realized in the space of the pop/off/art gallery in Moscow's Winzavod, a contemporary art hub, from September 13 to October 15, 2017, as part of the Parallel Program of the 7th Moscow International Biennale of Contemporary Art. *Battle of the Invalids* (right, p. 22, and pl. 28) takes place on a ground marked like a sports field and occupied by two teams of five players—papier-mâché figures based on ancient sculptures of a Japanese warrior and a Greek athlete and mounted on remote-controlled carts. Embodiments of Eastern and Western masculinity and military prowess, the original sculptures, from the collection of the Metropolitan Museum of Art in New York, are crippled by time with missing limbs.

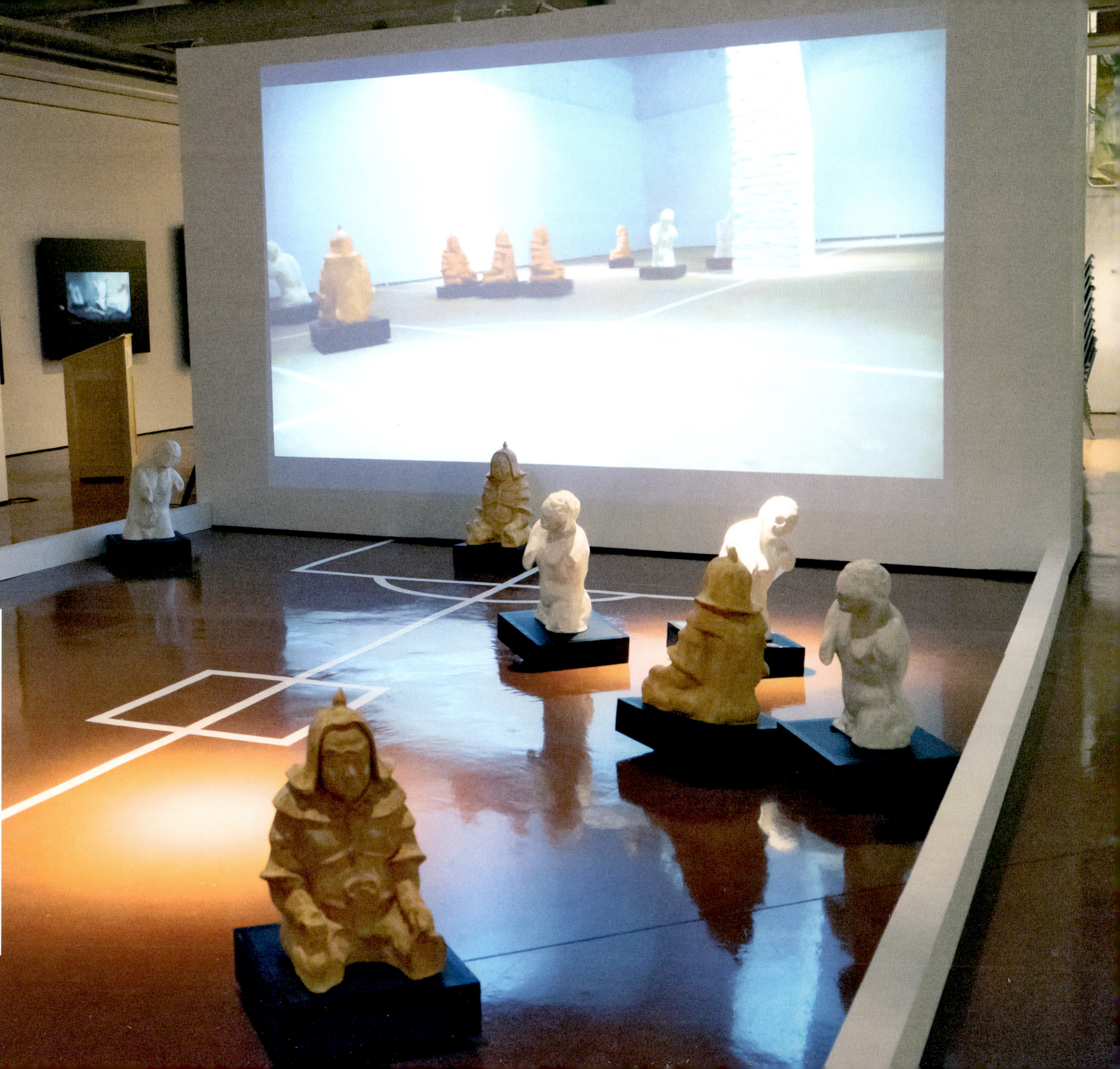

Battle of the Invalids, 2017, installation at Zimmerli Art Museum, 2019

As the gallery's space was transformed into a playground for an imaginary game, visitors were confined to the mezzanine of the upper gallery to observe the game while using joysticks to manipulate individual "players" to move, advance, or crash into the enemy players in this game with no rules or purpose or winners. The very nature of the interaction underscores the idea behind the project—to engage quintessential visual representations of two cultures, Eastern and Western, in a simulacrum of a war game conducted through mindless manipulation by outside forces disengaged from the actual battleground. While the 1980s *Rooms* "were not simply artistic environments that tested various regimes of visual perception, but addressed social allegory as well,"[6] *Battle of the Invalids* continues to address the issues of geopolitical transformation through the subtle, ironic, and playful theatricality evident in Nakhova's interactive projects throughout the 1990s and 2000s.

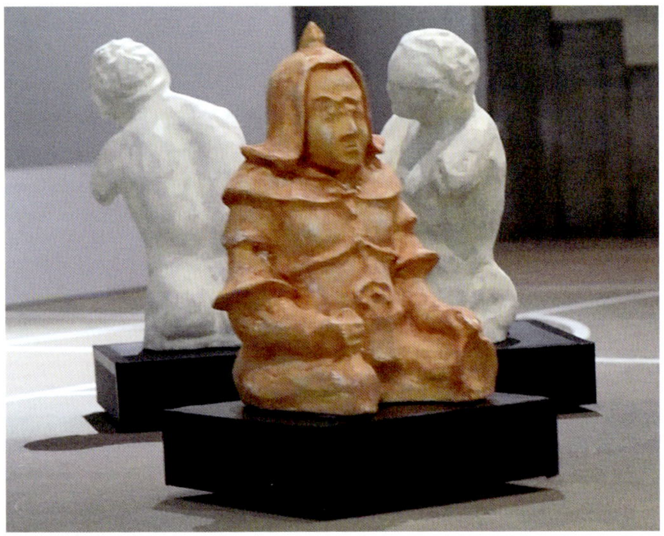

Battle of the Invalids, 2017. Courtesy pop/off/art gallery, Moscow.

The history of art has been one of Nakhova's sources of inspiration, though less in terms of a simple appropriation of imagery than of a superimposition of past and present that alters the interpretation of the former and the perception of the latter.[7] Nakhova has borrowed from sculptural forms of the past many times before, from the graveyard of monuments painted on camp beds (*Camping*, 1990, pl. 9) to the medieval *Queen* (1996, pls. 16, 17), a head and belly molded from papier-mâché and shrouded in silk that inflates into a phallic form when a viewer approaches. Nakhova used classical forms to explore the construction of gender "as a by-product of all cultural production . . . examining the interstices between process and completion, between fragmentation and wholeness, between the extant and the ruined."[8] In her reappropriation of the classical form, Nakhova has exposed the gender assumptions at its core. In *Battle of the Invalids*, she uses the same principle to reflect on another classic opposition—the East and the West.

The figures of *Battle of Invalids* are the result of a multistage process of visual selection, documentation, re-creation, and replication. From the entire collection of the Metropolitan Museum of Art, Nakhova chose the inconspicuous Greek sculpture *Small Marble Statue of an Athlete*[9] and a wooden carving of a Japanese guardian spirit, *Daishogun*,[10] both with missing limbs and damaged faces. In an interview she gave during the exhibition's run in Moscow, Nakhova commented: "In this Japanese sculpture, in addition to the ritual, there is much that is human, as in the sculpture from ancient Greece. It was important for me to find something human, to which the viewer and I can relate, so that a senseless battle between two cultures would be created."[11]

The process of replication and its significance are fully acknowledged by the artist, who engages in the discourse started by Walter Benjamin in the 1930s.[12] Her process is complicated to the point of irony, with the aim of ensuring that the resulting replicas (not copies) are not identical. She starts with photographic

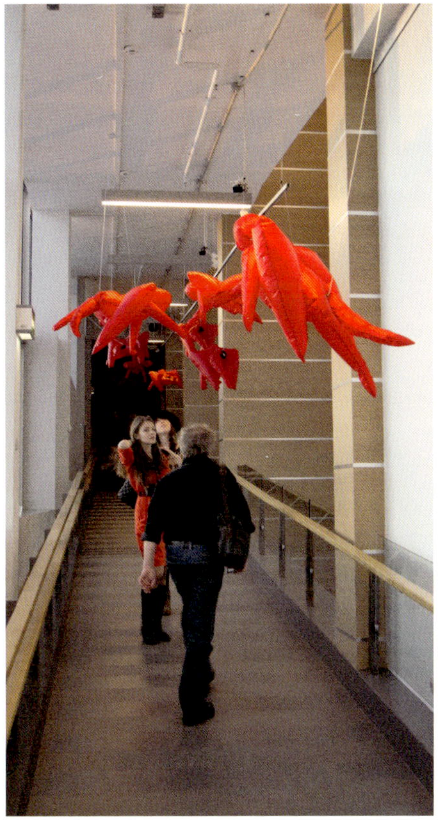

Annunciation: Red Angels, 2000. Installation at the Worker and Kolkhoz Woman Center, Moscow.

reproduction, taking pictures of the sculptures in their vitrines from various angles. Next come replicas hand-modeled in clay, followed by plaster casts, which, in turn, are followed by hollow papier-mâché figures. The result is two thin, light forms that can be replicated anywhere. Nakhova made one set to serve as a model for the production of four further sets. She enlisted help from professionals at a theater props workshop in Moscow, and in the end there were ten figures—five of each type, with the Japanese warriors painted a woody brown and the Greek athletes, a marble white. The judge of the tournament is an écorché torso after one modeled by Jean-Antoine Houdon in 1767 to represent the structure of human musculature, which was used for anatomical studies at art schools for generations. Nakhova can recall one plaster model from the Surikov Art Institute in Moscow that played an integral role in the education of Soviet art students. Through this process of replication, she continued to defy the notion of sculptural permanence paramount in traditional art history and education, just as she had previously done with her inflatable works (*Big Red*, 1998; and *Annunciation: Red Angels*, 2000, left and pl. 18) and wearable sculptures (*Friends and Neighbors*, 1994).

The figures, light and hollow, are set on remote-controlled toy cars. The game has no rules or clearly defined teams of players, and viewers are not made aware which figure they are controlling. The resulting Brownian motion leads to constant collisions and pointless conflict. For more than four decades, Nakhova has engaged her public in interactive games, immersing them in environments or engineering their engagement with sensor-activated mobile projects. She enjoys the drama and theatricality of her work. In *Battle of the Invalids*, she literally passes the control of the action to her public, underscoring the question of personal engagement and responsibility.

NOTES

1 Irina Nakhova, *Room No. 2*, 1984. Purchased with funds provided by the Russia and Eastern Europe Acquisitions Committee 2017. On display at Tate Modern Blavatnik Building throughout 2019, https://www.tate.org.uk/art/artworks/nakhova-room-no-2-t14789, accessed on January 1, 2019.

2 Joseph Backstein, discussions of *Rooms*, in *Sborniki MANI: Moskovskii Arkhiv Novogo Iskusstva* (Moscow: Biblioteka moskovskogo kontseptualizma Germana Titova, 2010), 201–308 (in Russian).

3 The video footage was courtesy of Sabine Hänsgen.

4 Sarah Cascone, "Ukrainian Activists Occupy Russia's Venice Biennale Pavilion," artnet News, May 8, 2015, https://news.artnet.com/exhibitions/ukraine-on-vacation-russian-pavilion-venice-295947, accessed on December 30, 2018.

5 Interview with Nakhova by Olga Danilkina, September 28, 2017, courtesy of the pop/off/art gallery, Moscow. Indeed, in the late 1980s and early 1990s, with the social fabric of the Soviet Union breaking up, soldiers, subjects of the universal conscription for males practiced during the Soviet regime, found themselves neglected by social services. Some of them were victims of the land mines used during the 1979–89 war in Afghanistan, one of the Cold War proxy conflicts of the late twentieth century. Beggars were controlled by the Mafia, organized and assigned territories in which to beg.

6 Margarita Tupitsyn, "The Russian World: A Hare or a Bear," in *Irina Nakhova: The Green Pavilion—Russian Pavilion, 56th International Art Exhibition, Venice Biennale*, exh. cat., ed. Margarita Tupitsyn (Cologne: König; Moscow: Stella Art Foundation, 2015), 35.

7 Helen Petrovsky, "The Art of Sensuous Concepts," in *Irina Nakhova: Rooms*, exh. cat., Moscow Museum of Modern Art, ed. Nelly Podgorskaya (Moscow: Maier, 2011), 27.

8 Jo Anna Isaak, *Feminism and Contemporary Art: The Revolutionary Power of Women's Laughter* (New York: Routledge, 1996), 116.

9 Greek, Hellenistic period, 3rd or 2nd century BC, marble, H. 17⅜ in. (44.1 cm), Rogers Fund, 1917,17.230.3.

10 Japan, Heian period, 11th–12th century, wood, H. 13½ in. (34.3 cm), Rogers Fund, 2017, 17.216.4.

11 Danilkina interview.

12 Walter Benjamin, "The Work of Art in the Age of Mechanical Reproduction," in *Illuminations*, ed. Hannah Arendt (New York: Schocken, 1968), 220.

GABRIELLA A. FERRARI

First Comes the Feeling: A Dialogue with Irina Nakhova

This text has been edited for clarity.

GABRIELLA FERRARI: With its wide-ranging selection of your works in a variety of media, *Irina Nakhova: Museum on the Edge* is partly a retrospective of your works. What does it feel like to have to select numerous works for a museum or a gallery exhibition? Do you feel as if you are managing your biography or a narrative of your life?

IRINA NAKHOVA: In this exhibition I have mainly chosen works of art that are here in the United States. I hadn't seen many of these artworks for fifteen to twenty years. While unpacking these works I felt as if I was looking into the past. But some of them are really very relevant even today. More recent pieces that I thought would be appropriate to the museum theme of this exhibition are *Gaze*, which was recently shown at the Pushkin Museum in Moscow; the *Vanitas* diptych; the painting *Kiss*; and the installation *Battle of the Invalids*, which I brought over with me in a suitcase, as I regularly do. My pieces are often nomadic works. I thought of them that way because I have been going back and forth between Russia and the United States since 1989. And I am always thinking about how I can manage to bring works across borders. That's how silk and inflatables came about. For travel purposes I could make large sculptures and still put them in my pocket. The most expensive part is to transport canvases in crates, of course. So I roll them and bring them with me as luggage. I am still doing the same thing that I was doing almost thirty years ago.

GF How does this exhibition differ from past displays of your work in the early years of your career in Moscow in the late Soviet period?

IN There were no exhibitions. And, strictly speaking, one can't even talk about having had an artistic career. This was unavailable to us unofficial artists in the Soviet Union. You just showed your work to your friends. You invited them to your apartment. Or, rather, they just showed up and came in. There were no cell phones, so sometimes you just dropped by and you didn't even call in advance. You showed up, you knocked on the door, and there were people there. They always seemed to expect you. It was a more flexible way of communicating and more in the moment.

GF What changed in the kinds of conversations about art that you have now?

IN What impacts the work now are the discussions with curators about the possibilities that are available for preparing a piece. If you are just working inside your apartment, you are a creator and curator of your own work and space. You are free to decide on anything; you are not impacted. That's why I miss the kind of work in which you do not have any communication with an institution, only with your fellow artists. The minute you start communicating with art institutions, it does have an impact on you and your work because there are certain restrictions. But I love challenges, and that is what keeps the work exciting and interesting. I like

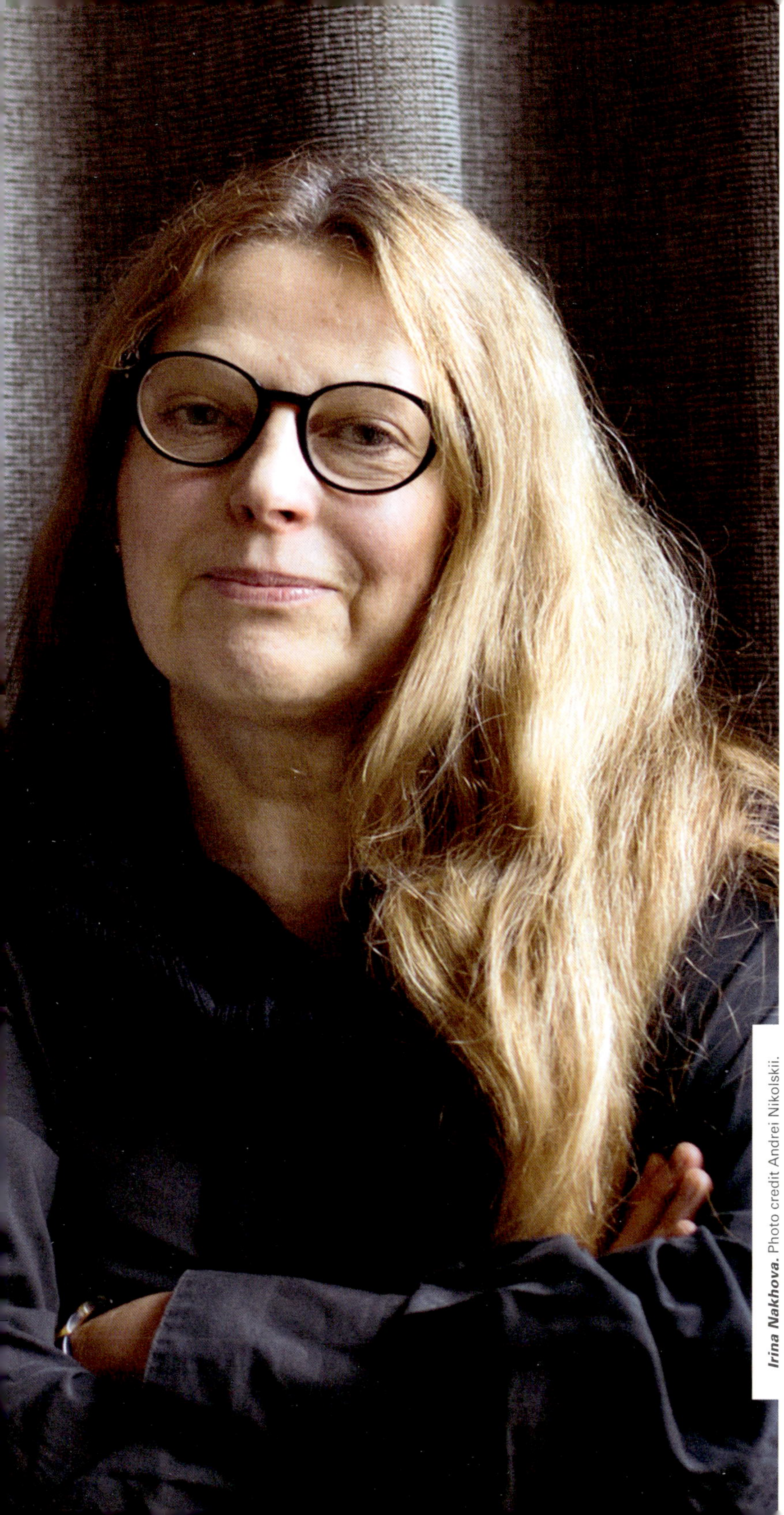

Irina Nakhova. Photo credit Andrei Nikolskii.

selecting works for an exhibition and thinking about how these will work in a very specific environment. When I am working with a museum and with art historical topics, I ask myself: "How can I impact this space? How can I make my installation work for me and for the museum as well?"

GF **The installation is a conversation piece with the environment in which it sits?**

IN Right, yes. But there are two different kinds of installation. In a curatorial installation I work with my own objects that are already made. This kind of project has its own challenges and its own creative aspects. In an art installation, on the other hand, the final piece emerges when the idea I have in my mind meets the space where it will be created. It is a dialogue between my vision and the environment that gives it form. Painting is another thing yet. Painting is a form of immediate work . . . with the material at hand. . . .

GF **The moment of encounter with the material is very important for you, yet you are also interested in technology and in the digital. You often work with screens and projections that combine, and sometimes clash, with handmade elements. Can you talk about how the digital and the manual parts of your work relate to one another?**

IN I think there is also a third element: painting. Painting belongs neither to the category . . . of digital nor to the one of craft. Painting is a way of processing time and my experiences in a different manner. With painting I am in a bubble. Nothing else exists around me. And I think that when I paint I gain time rather than waste it. Any kind of assemblage, or experiment with different materials and objects, and even sculpting to some extent, differs from painting because painting is an alternative reality in which I am not concerned with solving a puzzle. Unlike painting, other projects involve decision-making. They are also fun and exciting, but they are goal-oriented. When working on these projects, the use of different types of new technology for me always depends on an idea. It is all centered on . . . rendering a specific idea in the best possible way. For instance, when I was working in the 1990s on the inflatable sculpture of *Queen*, I was trying to figure out how to create the final effect. At that time I was teaching at Wayne State University and one of my students was an engineer by training. He helped me with that. I seek help when possible and then just do what I can on my own if I don't have any assistance.

GF **Is collaboration something that you value in your projects**?

IN John, my husband, always helps me. And I said to him that we do collaborate. But he says: "No, we don't collaborate. It's your idea and you use my help." He's probably right. Because collaboration for me is when I'm listening to somebody and then I might incorporate their idea into my work, if it makes it better.

GF Does the idea come first?

IN First comes the feeling: my mood. I do not remember the plot of a movie, for instance, but I remember my feelings about it. That's what makes it great. I remember the kind of feelings I experienced from a film or a book and their impact on me, not the story line. . . . I guess I am a feelings person, even though I am supposed to be a conceptualist! . . . What I am feeling in the moment is relevant or important to me, and it is tied to this particular time and environment. This comes first. I don't know where the idea comes from, but it somehow brews inside of me, from a feeling, from something deep. The material does not come first; it comes second. The idea comes first. Then I try to find the relevant material to embody this particular idea. I am flexible with the materials. It could be whatever suits the embodiment of a particular idea. If it needs painting, it will be painting. If the idea needs video, like *Gaze* did, I will work with video. If it requires sculpture, it will be sculpture. Over the years I've worked with different materials, and I picked them according to what I'd like to do. All the ideas come from life in one way or another, not from the material. I'm not attached to it. Painting, however, is a different process. I like painting because it clears my mind. But everything else depends on the idea.

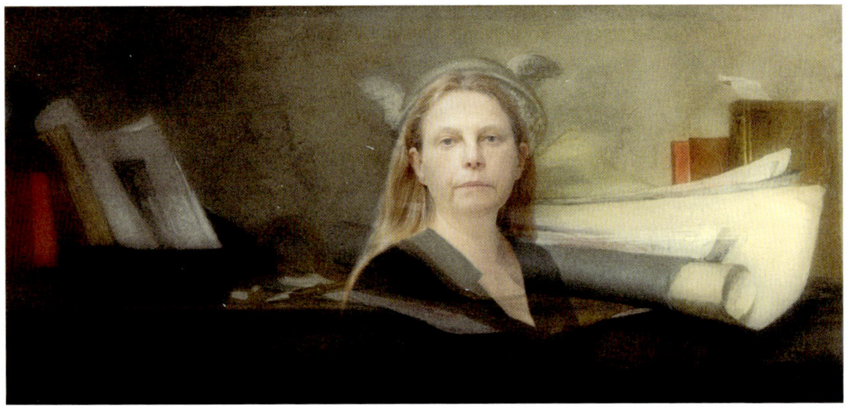

Gaze, 2016 (detail), video based on Chardin's *Still Life with Attributes of the Arts*, c. 1724–28

GF Your work draws on ideas about time: your biography, political and art history. What role does history play in your work?

IN History works as a general frame of reference. Take *Battle of the Invalids*, for instance. It was 2016 when I made the piece, but I was dealing with torsos and sculptures maimed by time already in the 1990s. The idea somehow came back in the 2000s, and it is a constantly recurring theme. People again are being crippled in wars as they were back then. The 1980s and 1990s were also kind of a rupture moment (*perelomny moment*). It was a big change, when we shifted from Soviet reality to the Russian one. We witnessed the collapse of a whole country and understood how quickly the building and crumbling of an empire can occur. For Soviet citizens this happened almost in the course of a single life span. During that time, I probably was not rationally aware that the system was finally broken. Yet, even then I had the feeling that organic life and the life of a political structure can both be very short. Somehow this resonated with my work on *Battle of the Invalids*.

GF In your work, the two-dimensional and the three-dimensional tend to have moments of encounter. For example, several of your paintings have layers that render them three-dimensional. Even the flattest of surfaces often contains the element of space and touch. How do your spatial works relate to your two-dimensional works?

IN I think there are two different types of painting. The works in the *Eyes* series, for instance, were objects for an installation. When flat surfaces become part of an installation, they do not work as pure paintings. They work as three-dimensional objects in space. I was a painter to begin with. Then my paintings grew bigger and bigger and I also started making them in series. Even early on, the paintings that hung in my Moscow apartment were relatively big and sometimes I could not even see them in their entirety. Increasingly, they became spatial constructions that I could assemble, rather than windows into a fantasy world. That's how my work gently evolved into three-dimensional installations. Even little objects within the paintings became markers of space. All the architectural details in them were spatial references. That's how the jump into making the *Rooms* series came about. However, the paintings that I make now are not related to three-dimensional space. They relate to my inner space. For instance, the *Vanitas* diptych is not related to space per se. Rather, they express an inner cultural environment.

GF **Some of your paintings strike me as being corporeal. They tend to engage the senses. Scale often draws the viewer into the fleshiness of your canvases. Surfaces become connective tissue between the viewer and the work. How important is the act of layering in your work?**

IN Yes, it is very important. Layering multiplies meaning and lends a certain degree of freedom to the viewers in their interpretation and perception of my work. I started using this technique quite a long time ago, actually. I made a series of paintings with stickers applied onto the surface of the canvas, like a double skin. Often revealing the blankness underneath. There were even some paintings from the 1980s where I left the canvas untouched. There were paint fragments in them that marked the fake reality of the painting as object. Even though I was not thinking of this at the time of making it, the series *Skins* also engages with the notion of fake reality. There we have the fake reality of the written story and fake reality of the material that emulates skin but is in fact a sheet of latex. And of course with *Skins*, first the idea was embodied in the written story. The latex prints were secondary to the texts. But it is the layering of text and image that creates the final piece.

GF **How much do you take into account the visitor as you prepare your installations?**

IN I never try to predict what the visitor or the onlooker may think about my work. Especially in installations, I want to be as open as possible so that there is no certainty in anything. I am entertaining myself in some ways; playing with all those elements. Investigating my own senses has always been amusing for me, somehow. I like playing tricks on a person. Maybe because for me it's always interesting to find something new, and it's only through this kind of play that I give myself an opportunity to test these things. If I sometimes have feedback from people who see my work, the interpretations of it are always so vastly different and so unpredictable.

GF **What is the relationship between the experience of imaginary worlds and reality in your work?**

IN I want to create some kind of space where people can encounter reality anew through their senses. I want to build places in which people can see something new for themselves or think about different things that probably never occurred to them, but are real all the same. There's so much fake reality outside, so anything that brings you back to reality is very important. Earlier, artists were dealing with fantasy worlds and bringing their spectators to something else, to different realities, expanding their worlds. Now, it looks like we need the opposite.... You need to come back from this expanded reality to the reality that is right here, like the surface of this table.... It's needed in our world. We need to come back to the ground. We need to come back to our senses.

GF **In this project of bringing us back to our senses, how important is the tool of laughter?**

IN I think laughter comes more or less naturally to it. I think it's just another tool to bring people back to reality, because with laughter you start thinking and processing. Sure, laughter can provide relief from burdens. But it also makes you think about things in a paradoxical manner. In doing so it brings you back to reality. Perhaps this is tied to the uncertainty of each next step in making and experiencing a piece of art. If something feels uncertain, it usually provokes laughter in me.

GF **But it can be scary as well.**

IN Yes, but scary elements are more primordial and they are less interesting. When something looks uncertain, laughter gives you room for more types of different reactions than if you were just scared. If you are scared, you don't want to encounter anything new at all. But with laughter you're not certain about your relationship to it.

GF **Uncertainty is clearly a key feature of your work. But how do you decide when a work is finished?**

IN When I was younger, I had the problem of overworking canvases. But now I have this problem less and less. With paintings I just know when I'm finished. I am done when I can't do anything else to the canvas. I never stop when I don't like what's happening in the painting. I sometimes paint and repaint the same surface. This is true of video too. The notion of layering is important to both painting and video. In them it is the overlapping of multiple layers that draws out something from deep within the work and makes it complete. Generally, however, I would say that I don't know in advance when a work is finished. I can only recognize it when I see it right in front of me. It's just a feeling.

Plates

1

Untitled, 1978
Four-part work
Oil on canvas
Each part: 13 1/16 × 16 1/4 in. (33 × 41 cm)
Overall: 26 3/16 × 32 1/2 in. (66.5 × 82.5 cm)
Norton and Nancy Dodge Collection of Nonconformist Art from the Soviet Union
ZIMMERLI ART MUSEUM

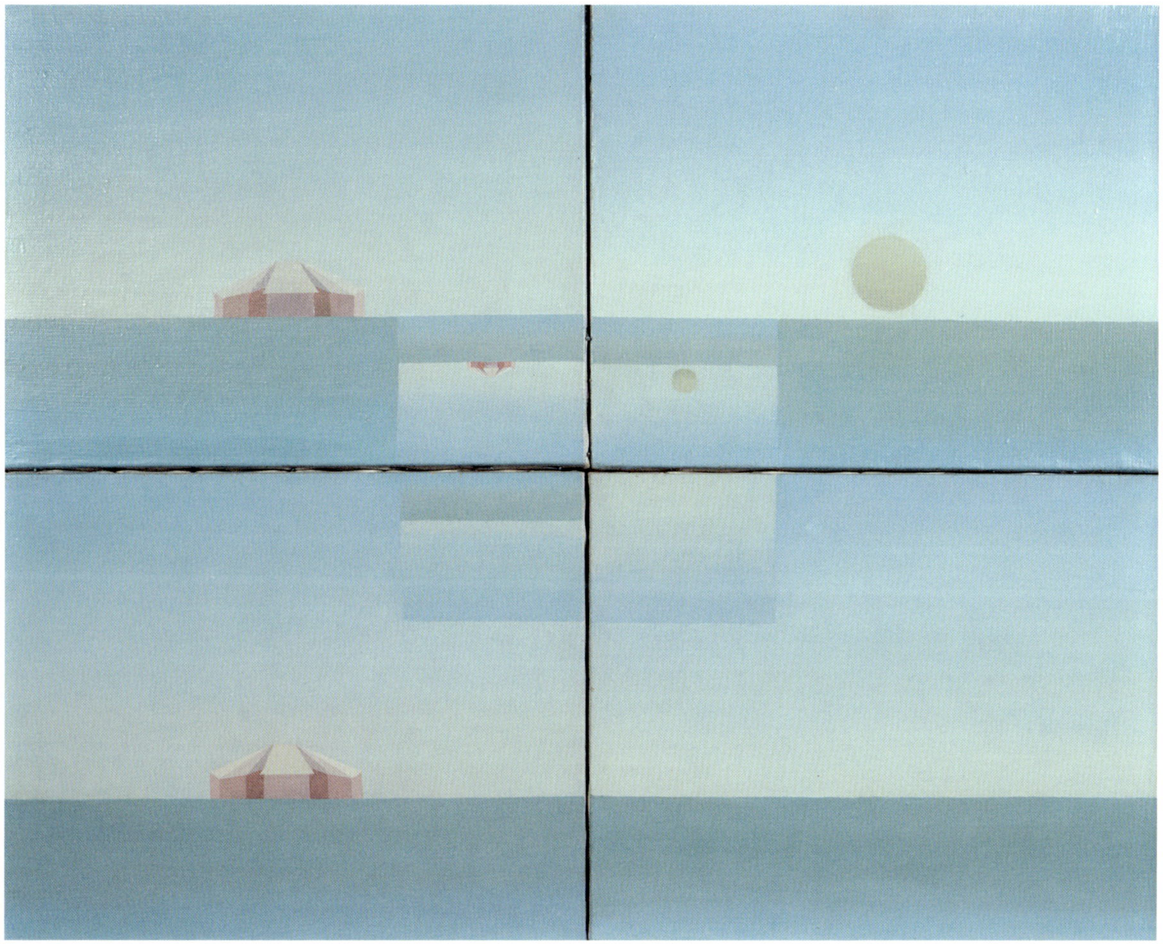

2

Room No. 1, 1983
Gelatin silver prints on paper
Each: 11⅛ × 13⅞ in. (28.2 × 35.3 cm)
Norton and Nancy Dodge Collection of
Nonconformist Art from the Soviet Union
ZIMMERLI ART MUSEUM

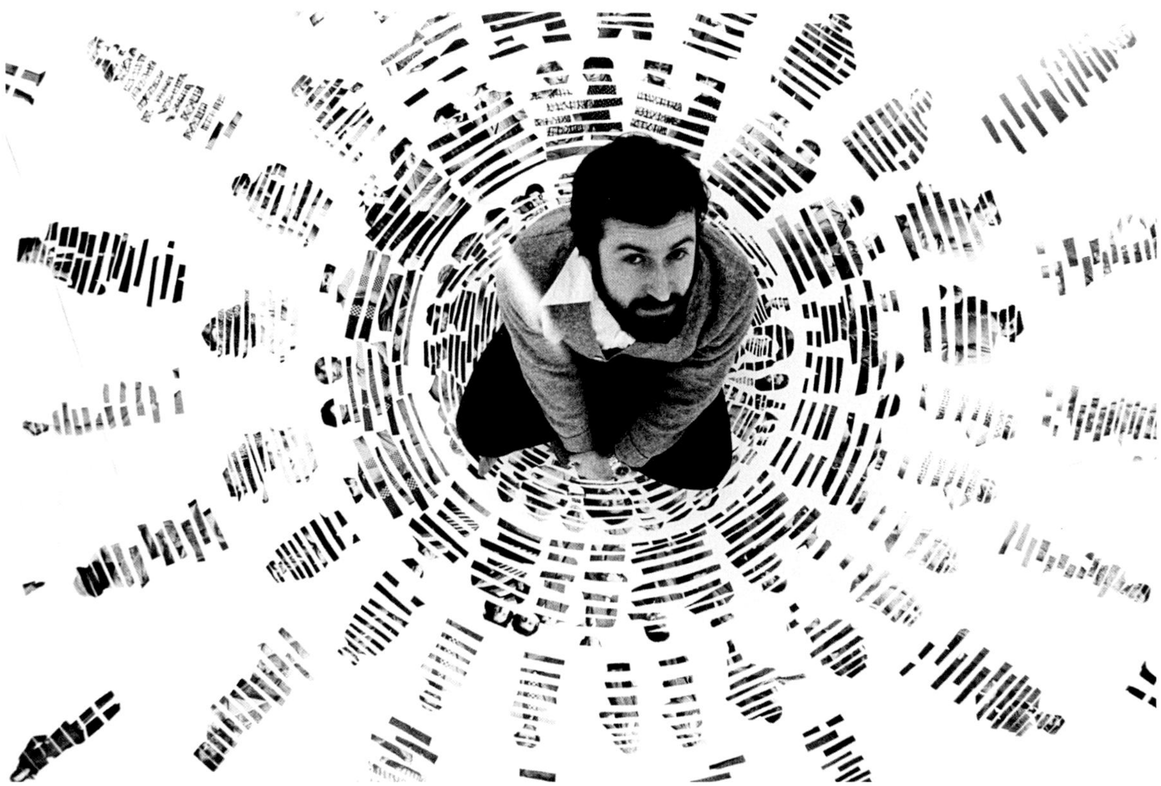

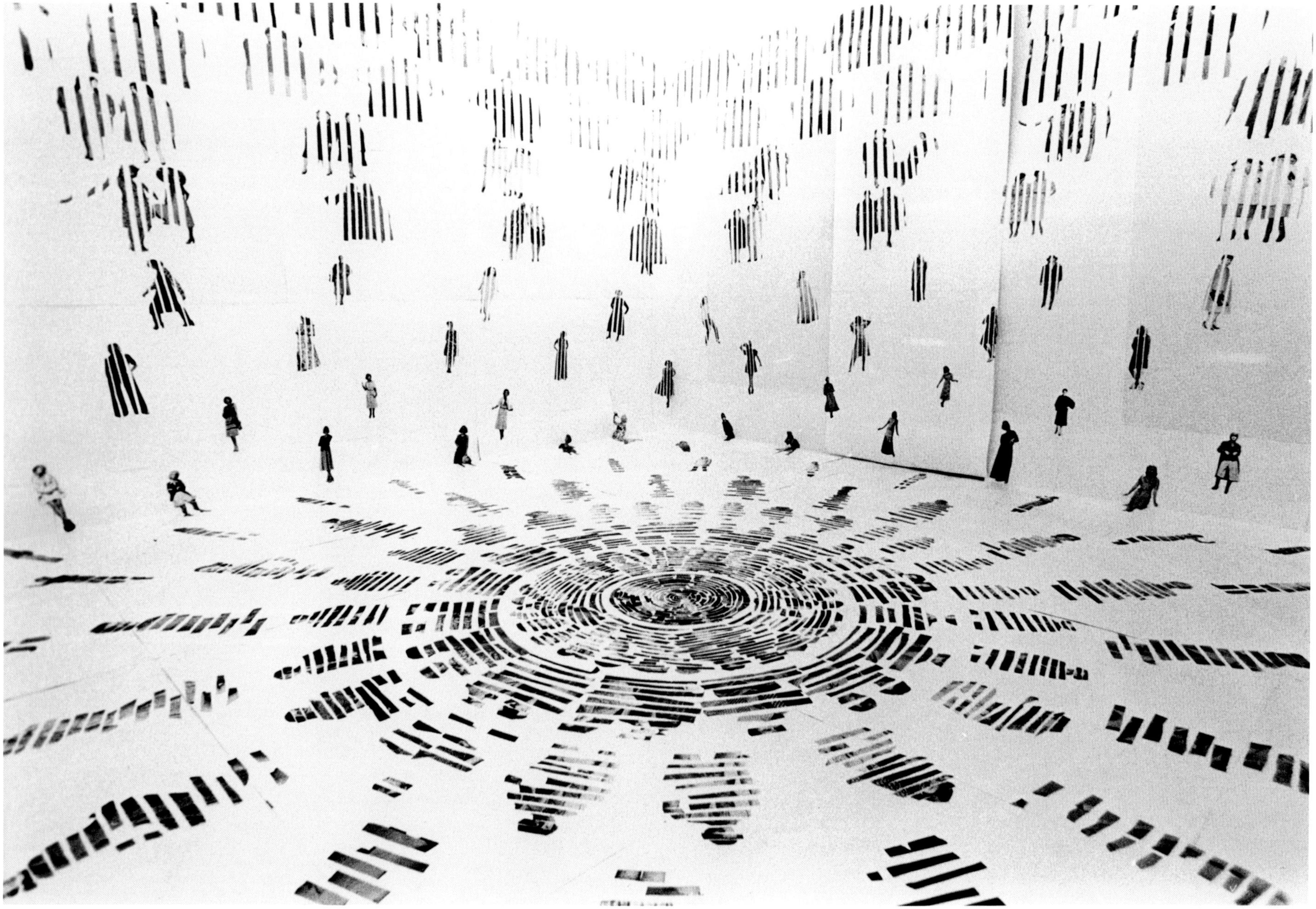

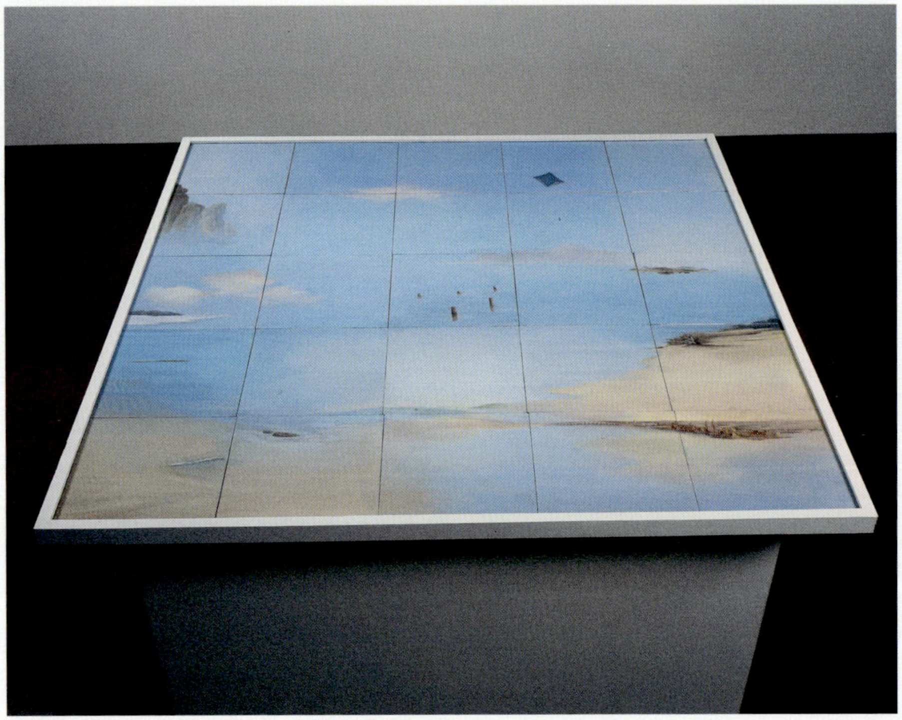

3

Variable Landscape, 1983
Twenty-five panels
Oil on gessoed Masonite
Each: $9\frac{13}{16} \times 9\frac{13}{16}$ in. (25 × 25 cm)
Norton and Nancy Dodge Collection of
Nonconformist Art from the Soviet Union
ZIMMERLI ART MUSEUM

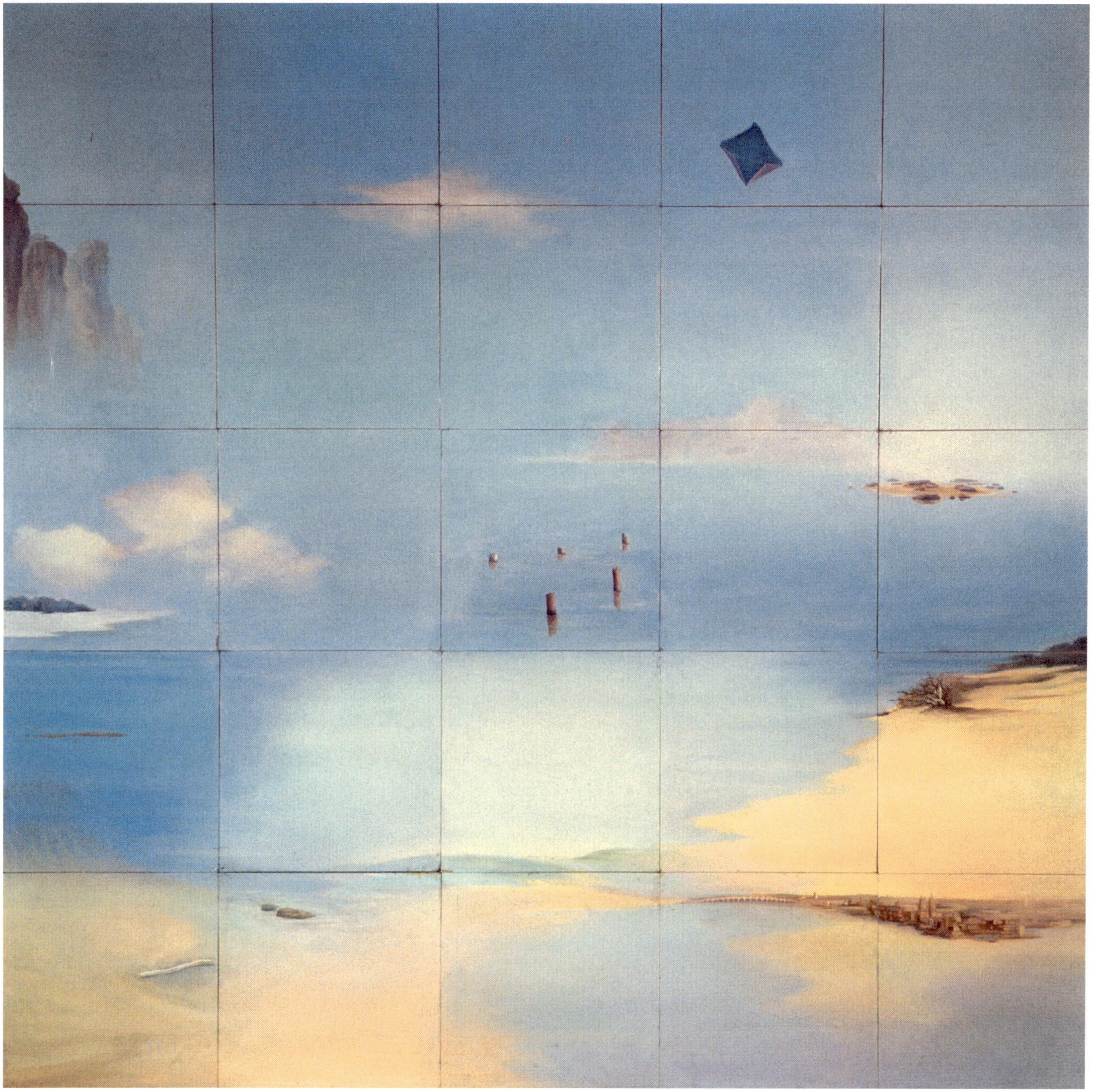

4

***Room No. 2*, 1984**
Gelatin silver prints on paper
Each: $11\frac{1}{16} \times 13\frac{15}{16}$ in. (28.1 × 35.4 cm)
Norton and Nancy Dodge Collection of Nonconformist Art from the Soviet Union
ZIMMERLI ART MUSEUM

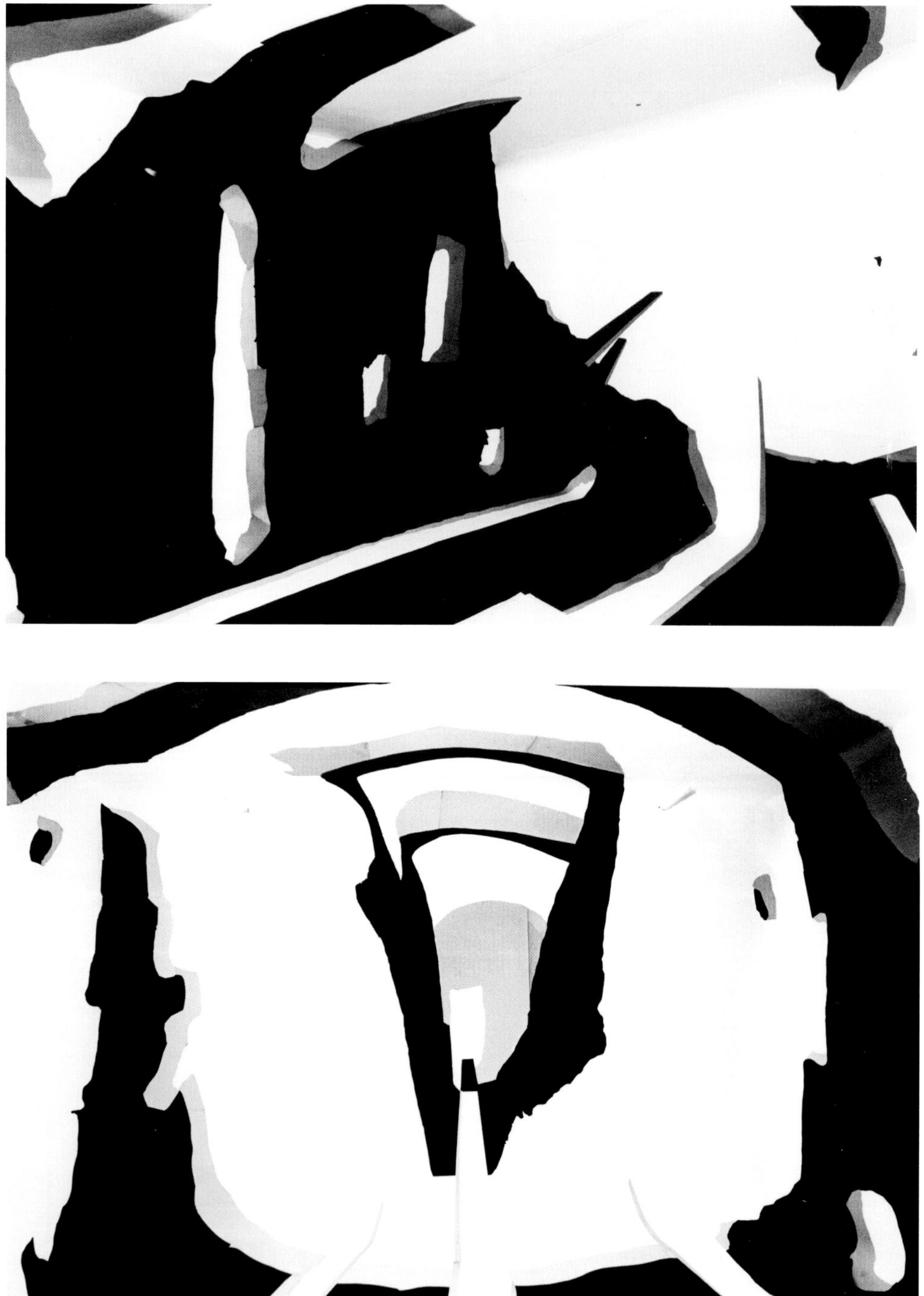

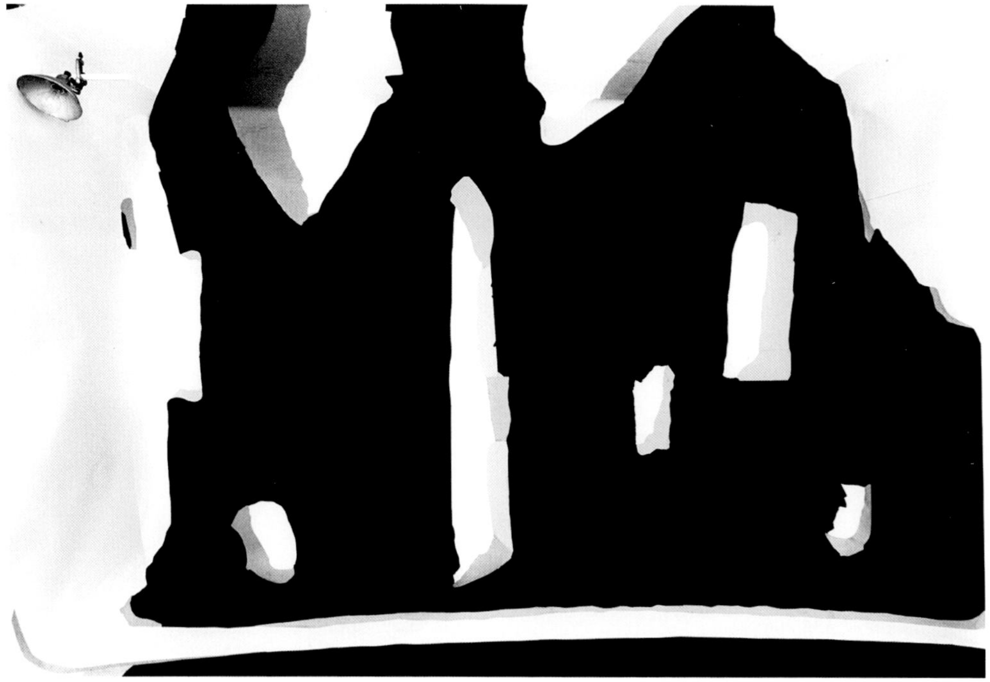

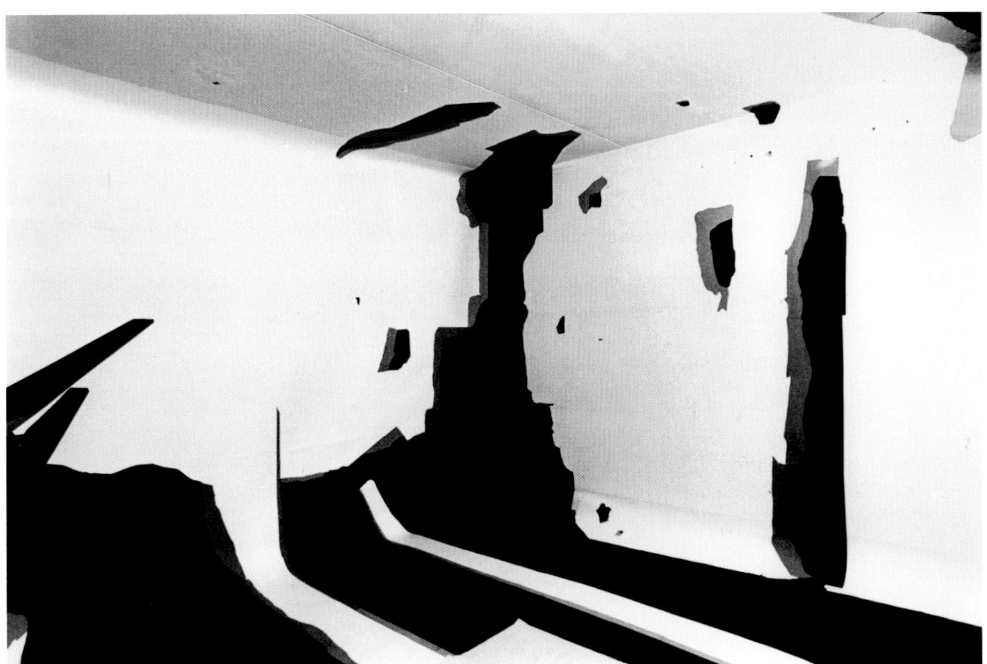

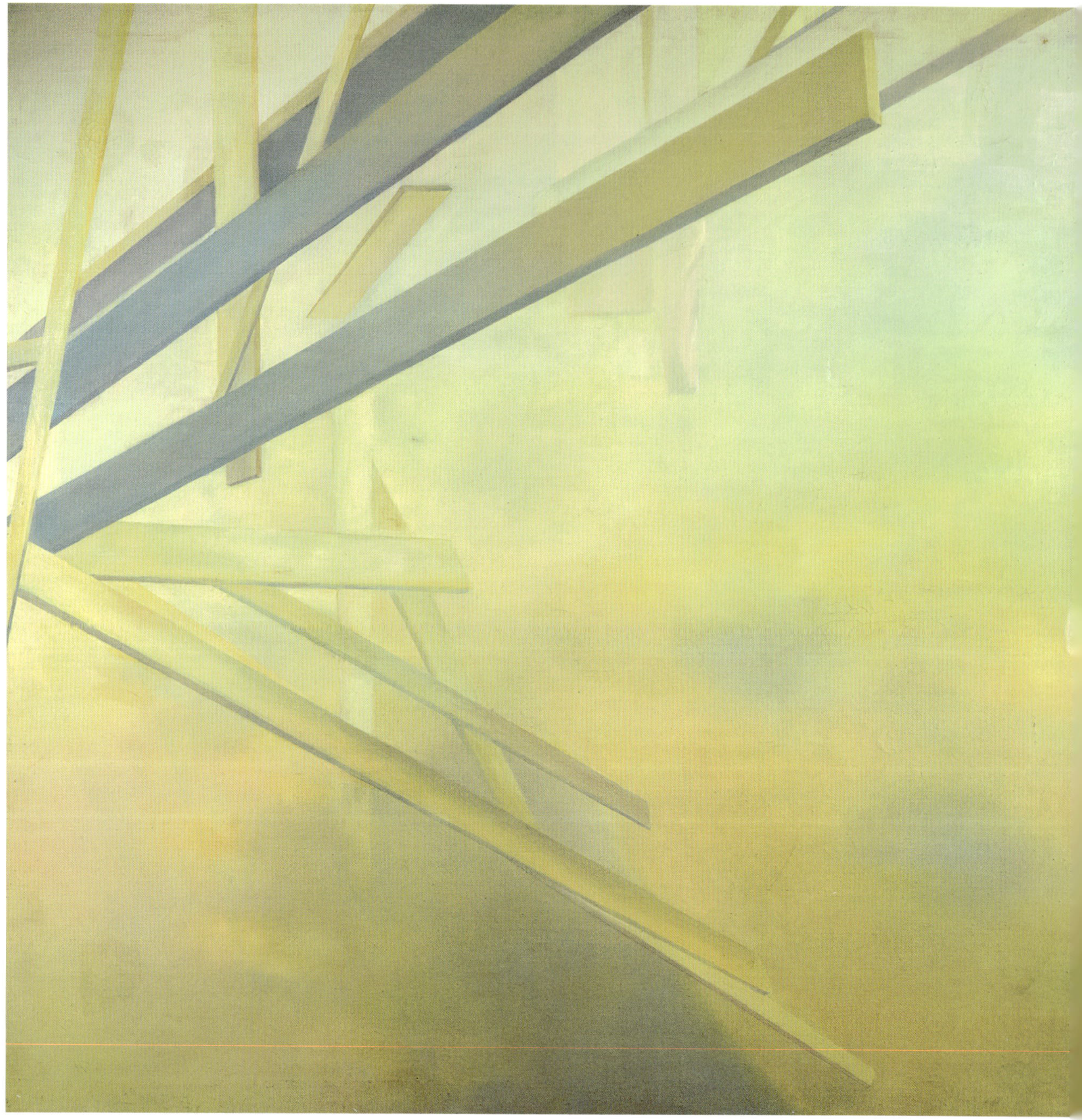

5

Scaffolding, 1984
Diptych
Oil on canvas
Each: 59 × 59 in. (150 × 150 cm)
Norton and Nancy Dodge Collection of
Nonconformist Art from the Soviet Union
ZIMMERLI ART MUSEUM

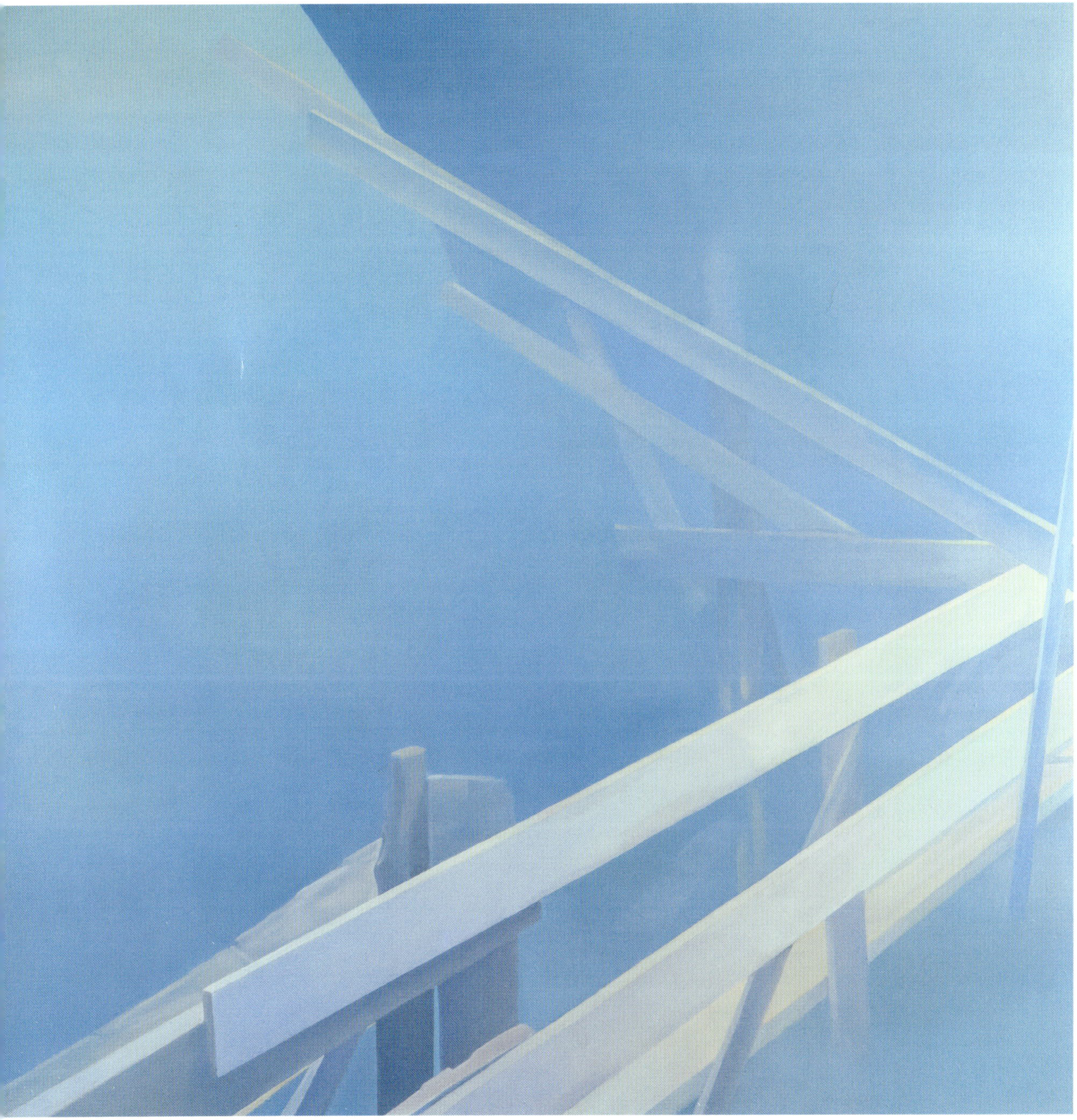

6

Five untitled collages, 1985
Collage, newspaper, gouache, and watercolor
Each: 18 15/16 × 14 3/16 in. (48 × 36 cm) or
14 3/16 × 18 15/16 in. (36 × 48 cm)
Norton and Nancy Dodge Collection of
Nonconformist Art from the Soviet Union
ZIMMERLI ART MUSEUM

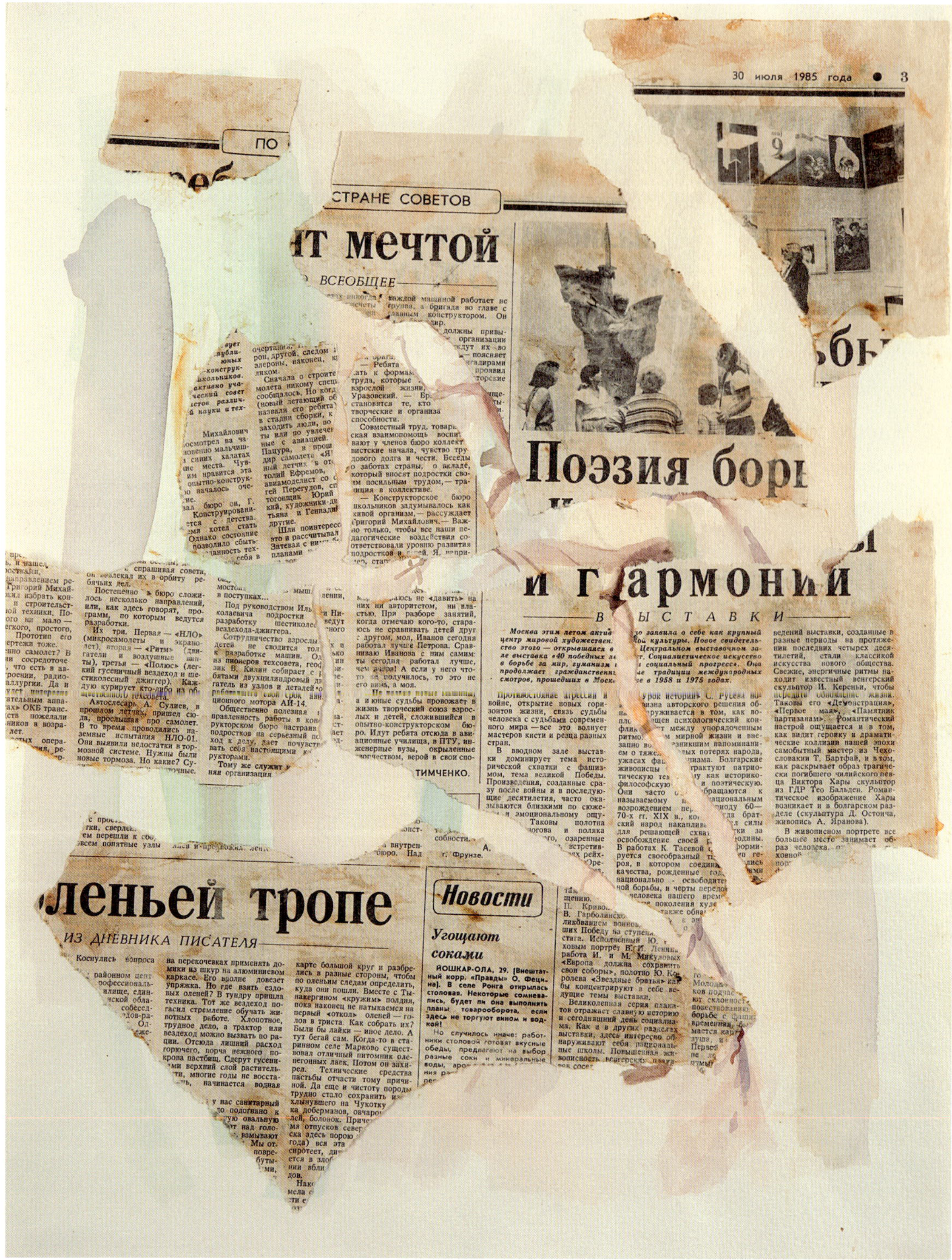

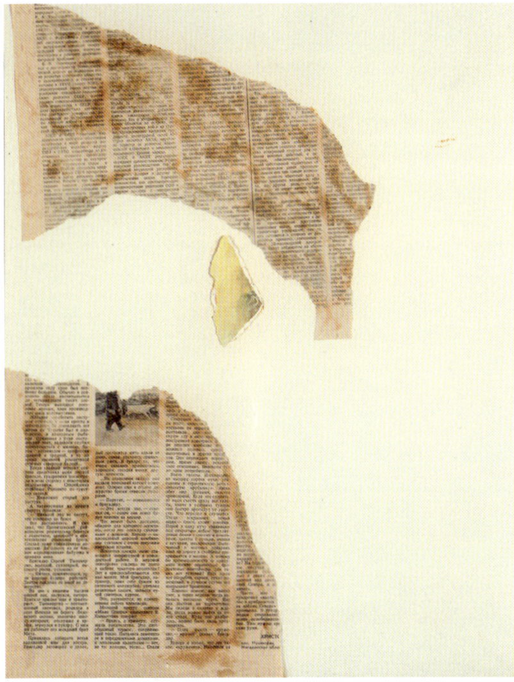

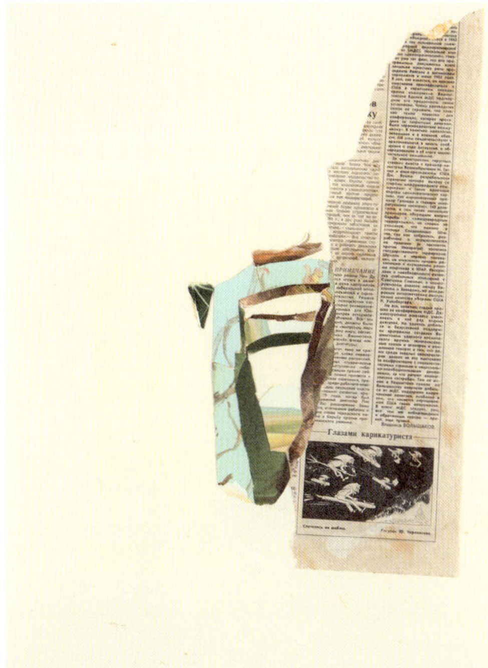

Глазами карикатуриста

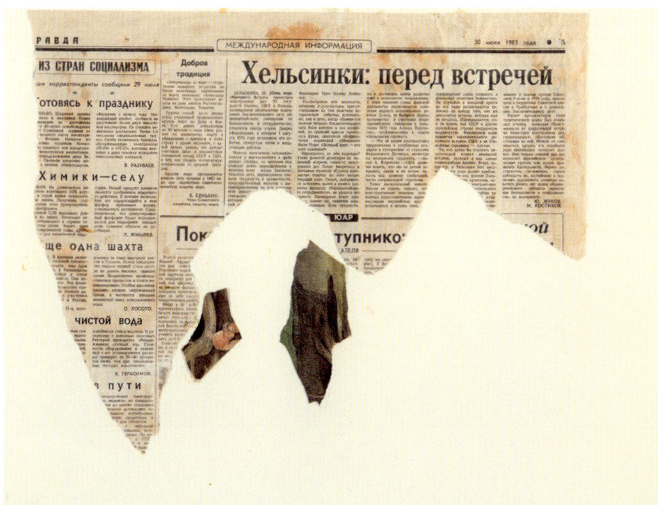

МЕЖДУНАРОДНАЯ ИНФОРМАЦИЯ
ИЗ СТРАН СОЦИАЛИЗМА
Доброе традиция
Хельсинки: перед встречей
Готовясь к празднику
Химики—селу
ЮАР
ще одна шахта
чистой вода

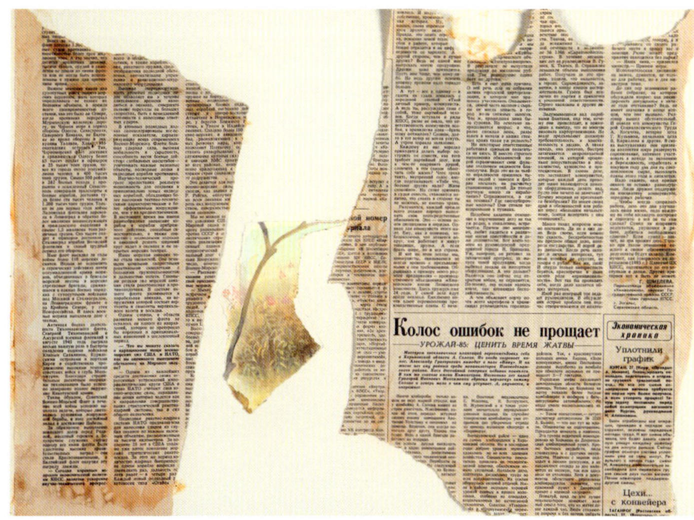

Колос ошибок не прощает
УРОЖАЙ-85: ЦЕНИТЬ ВРЕМЯ ЖАТВЫ
Экономическая хроника
Уплотнили график
Цехи... с конвейера

7

Room No. 4, 1986
Gelatin silver prints on paper
Each: 11⅛ × 13⅞ in. (28.2 × 35.3 cm)
Norton and Nancy Dodge Collection of
Nonconformist Art from the Soviet Union
ZIMMERLI ART MUSEUM

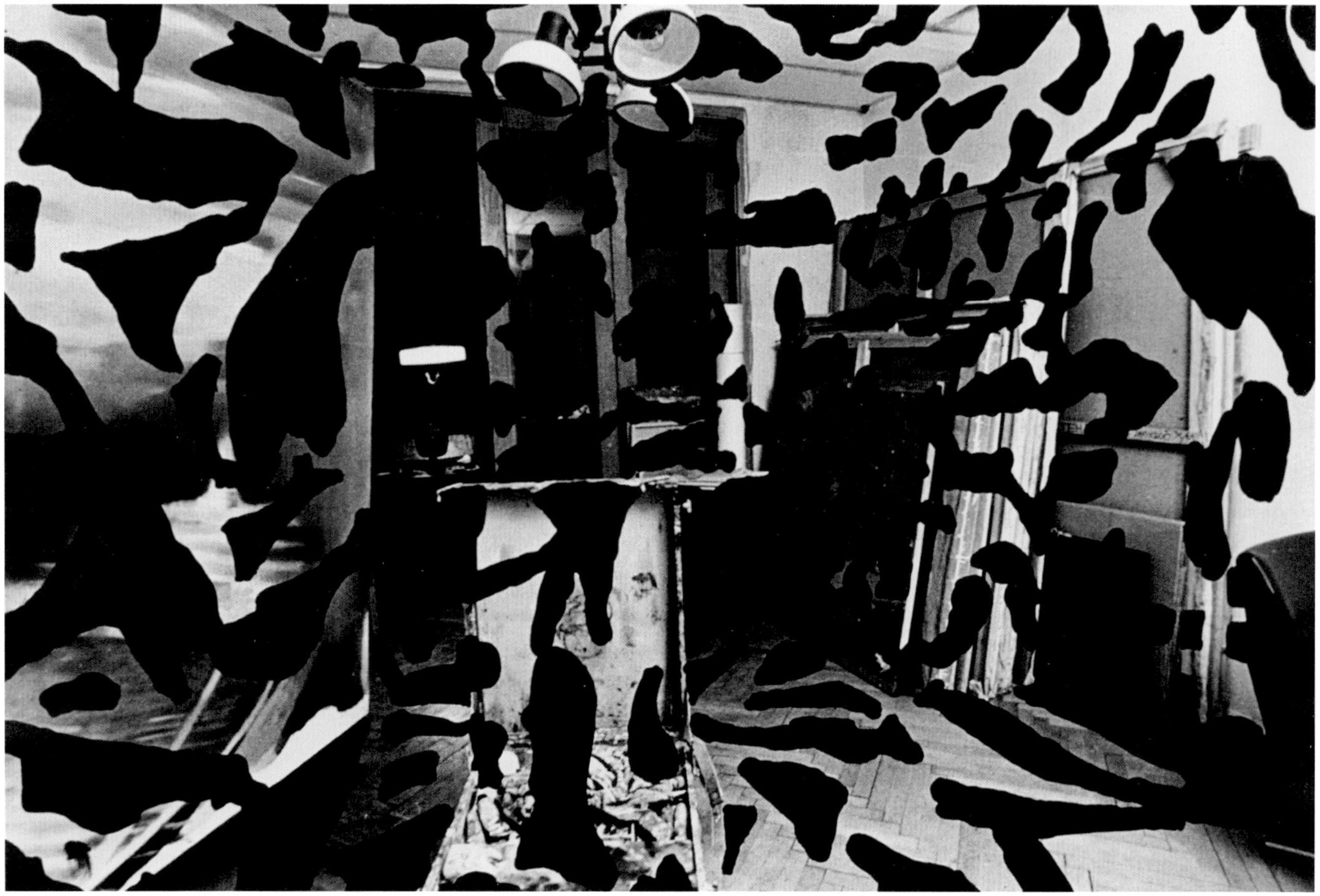

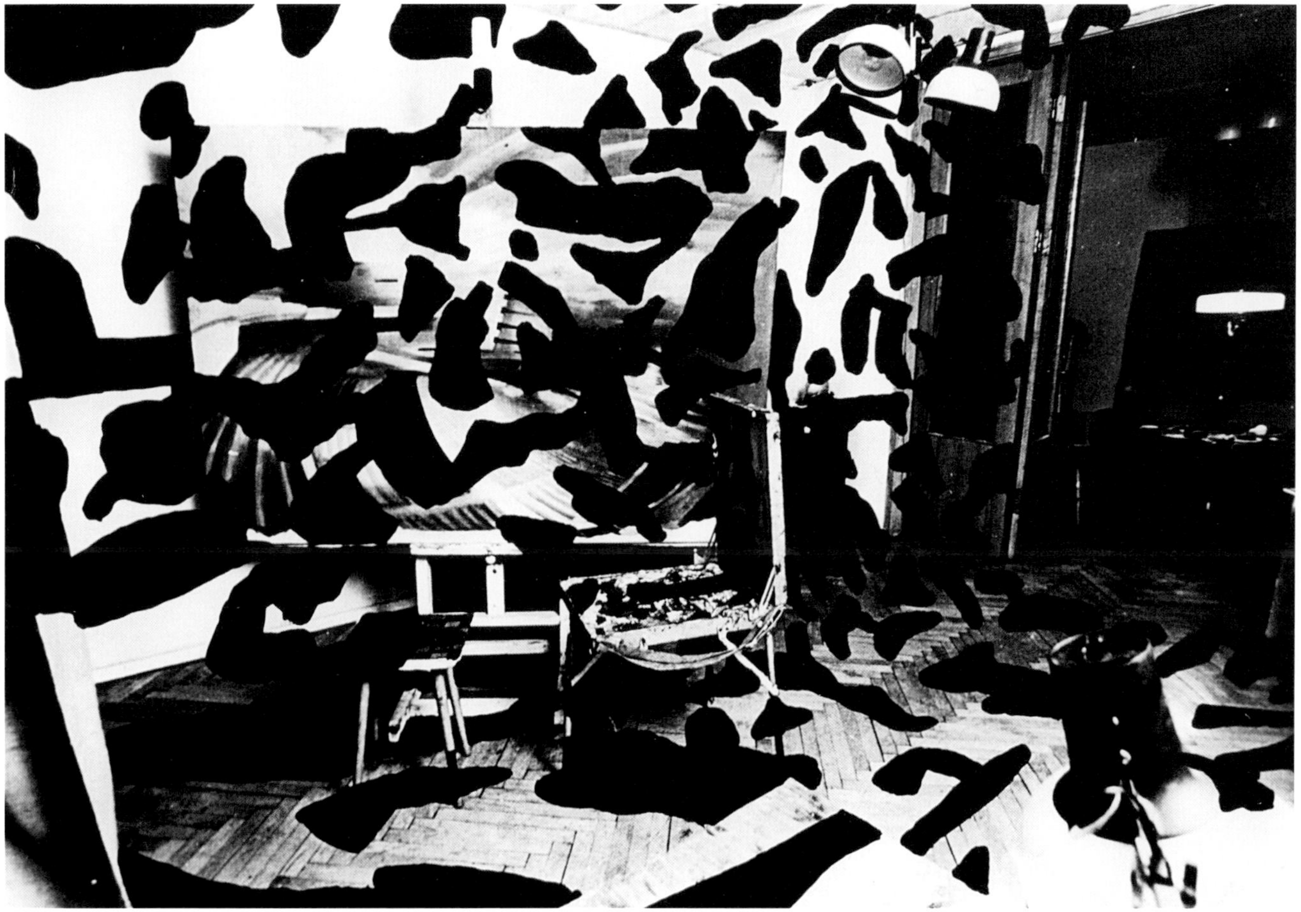

8

Double Vision, 1988
Polyptych, four panels
Acrylic and oil on canvas
Each: 59 × 78¾ in. (150 × 200 cm)
COLLECTION OF THE ARTIST

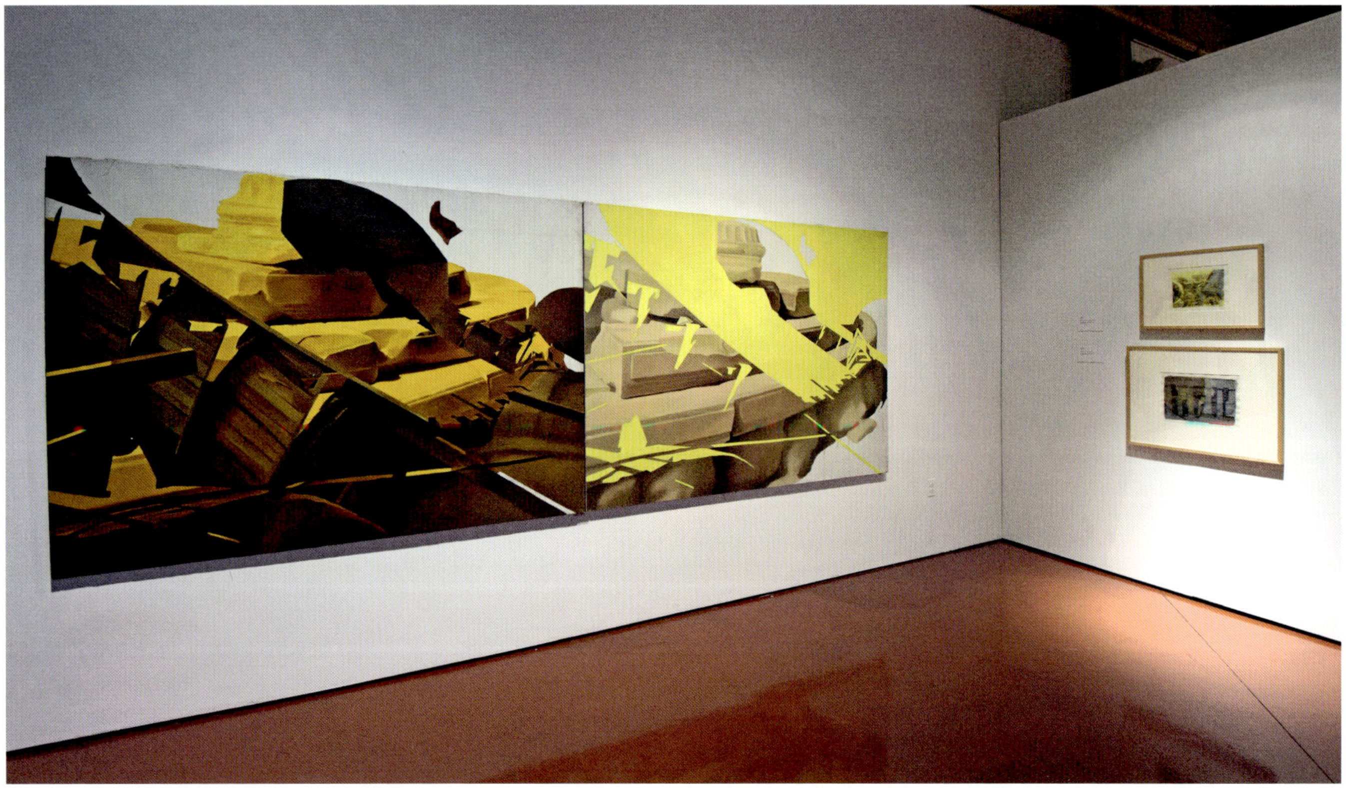

Double Vision, two of four panels, installation at Zimmerli Art Museum, 2019

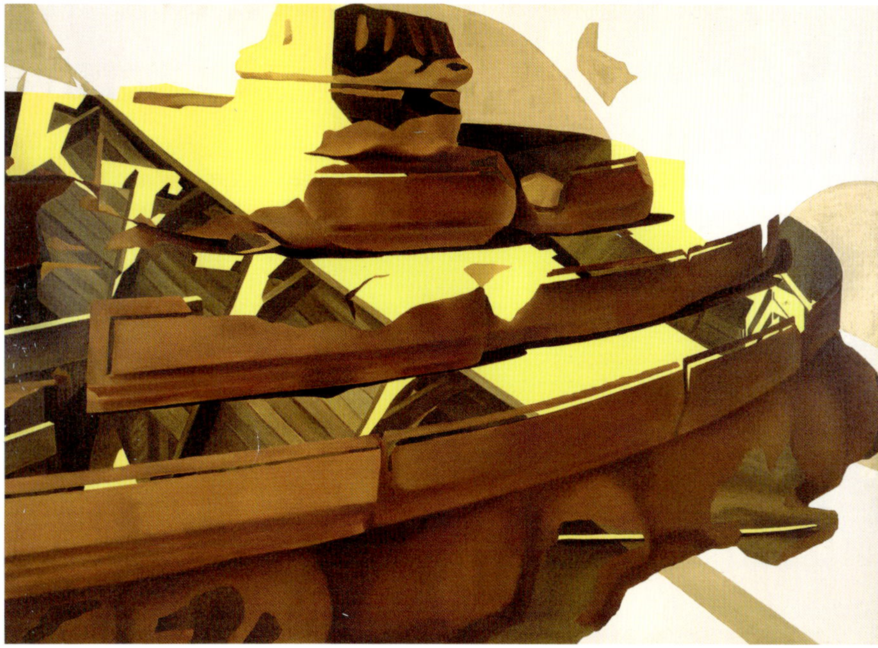

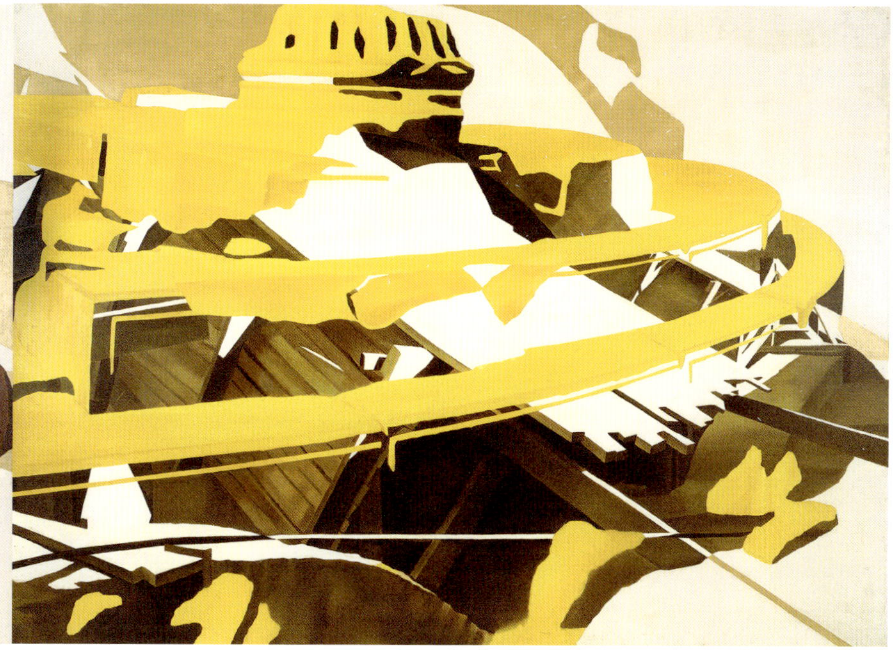

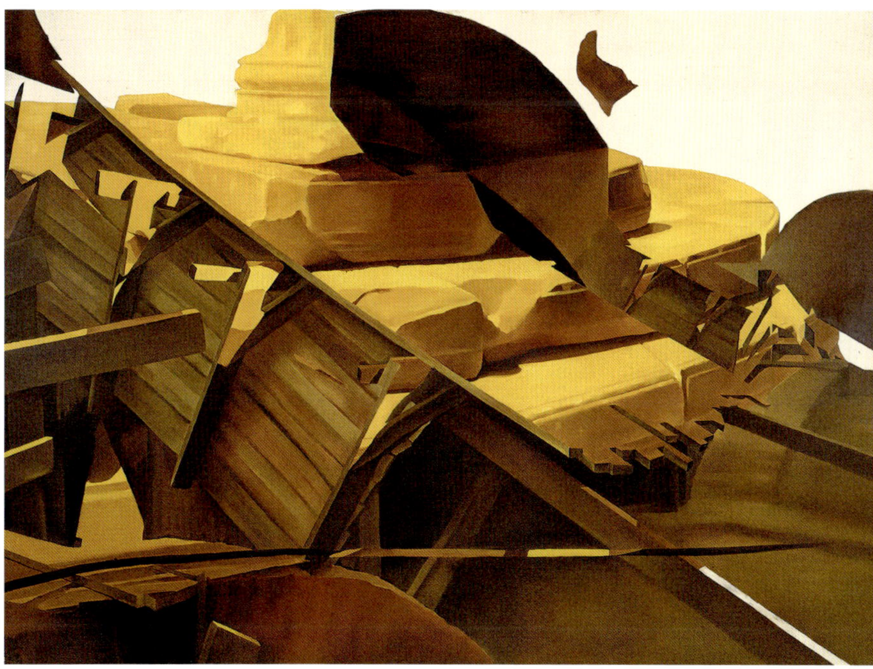

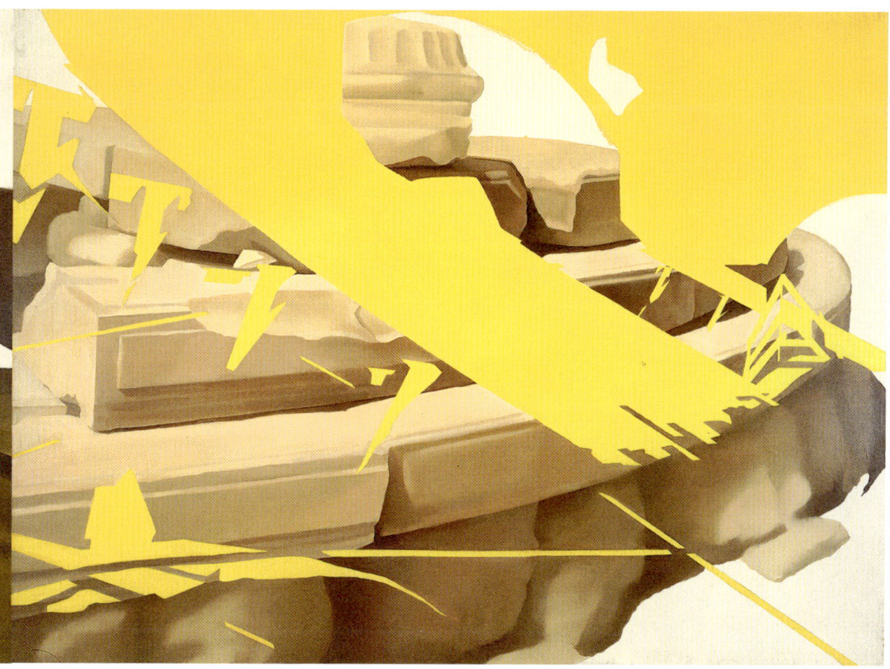

9

Camping, 1990

Acrylic and oil on canvas, army cots

Each: 78 × 28½ × 15 in. (198 × 72 × 38 cm)

Four from the series:

Three: COLLECTION OF THE ARTIST

One: Gift of Vals Osborne and José Moreno-Lacalle

ZIMMERLI ART MUSEUM

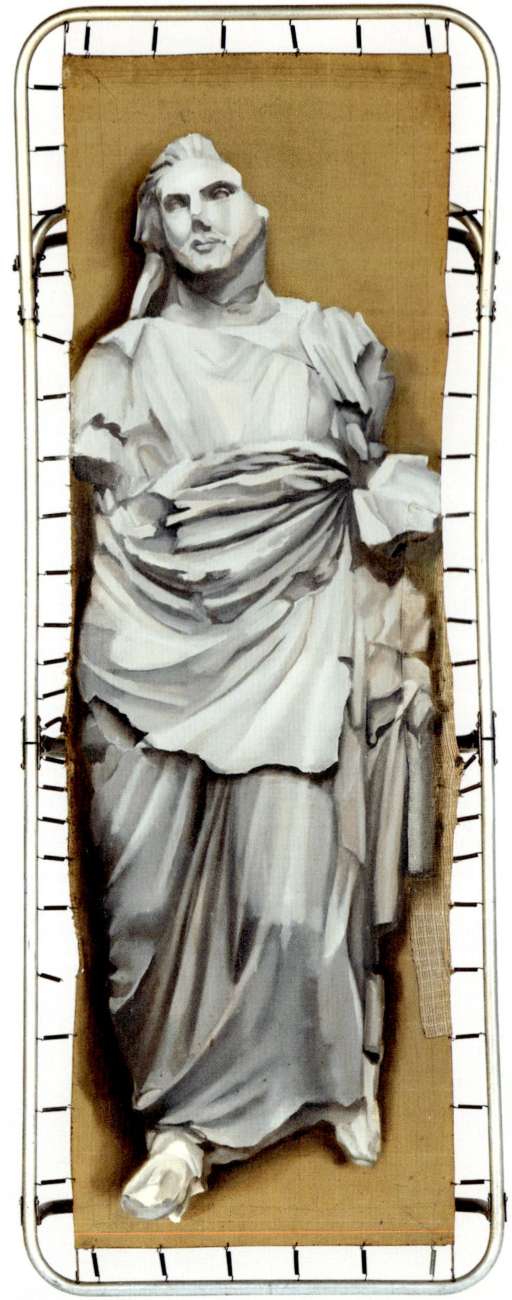

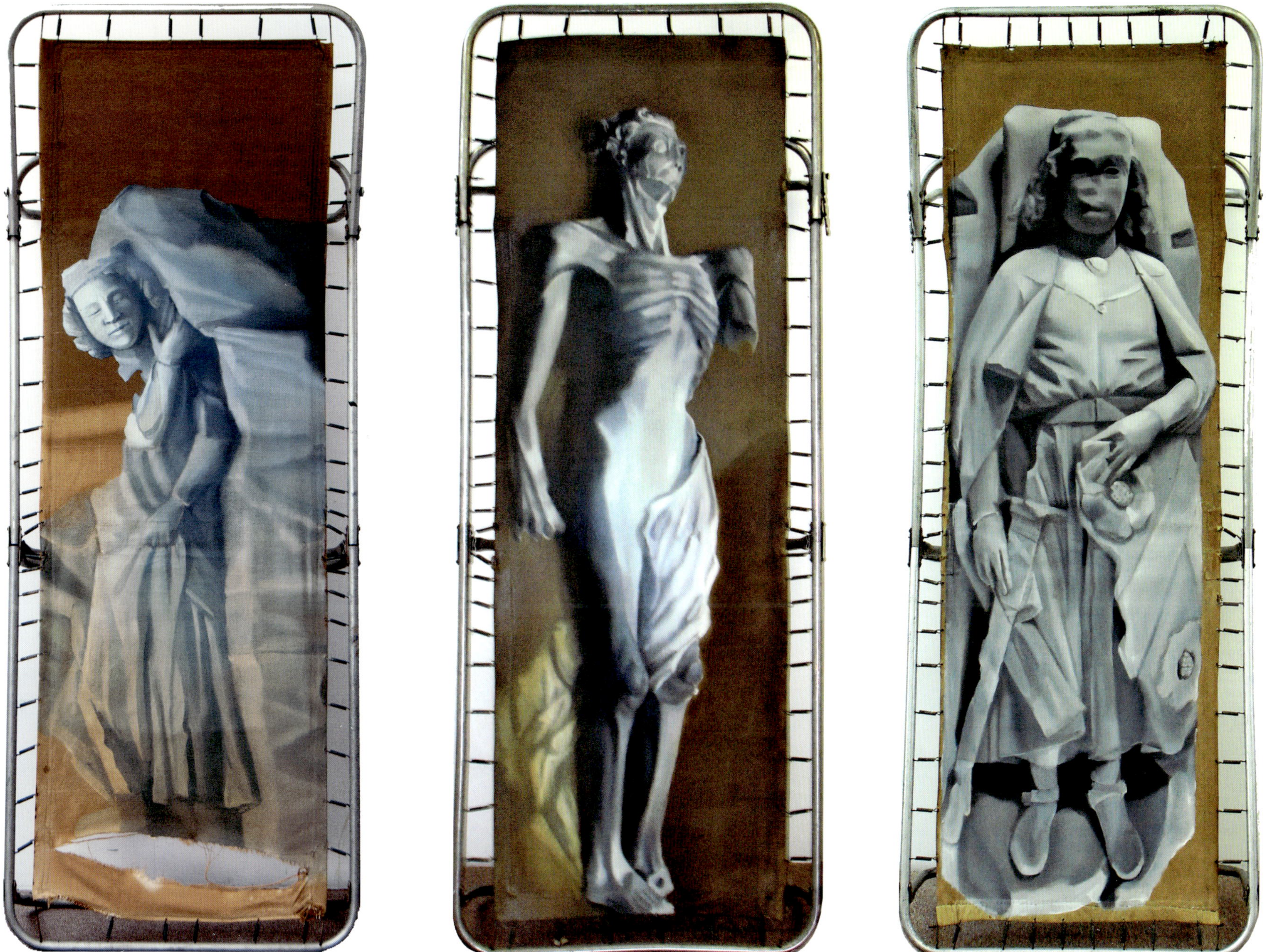

10

Mobeus, 1990
Diptych
Acrylic and oil on shaped canvas
Overall: 49 × 156 in. (124 × 396 cm)
COLLECTION OF THE ARTIST

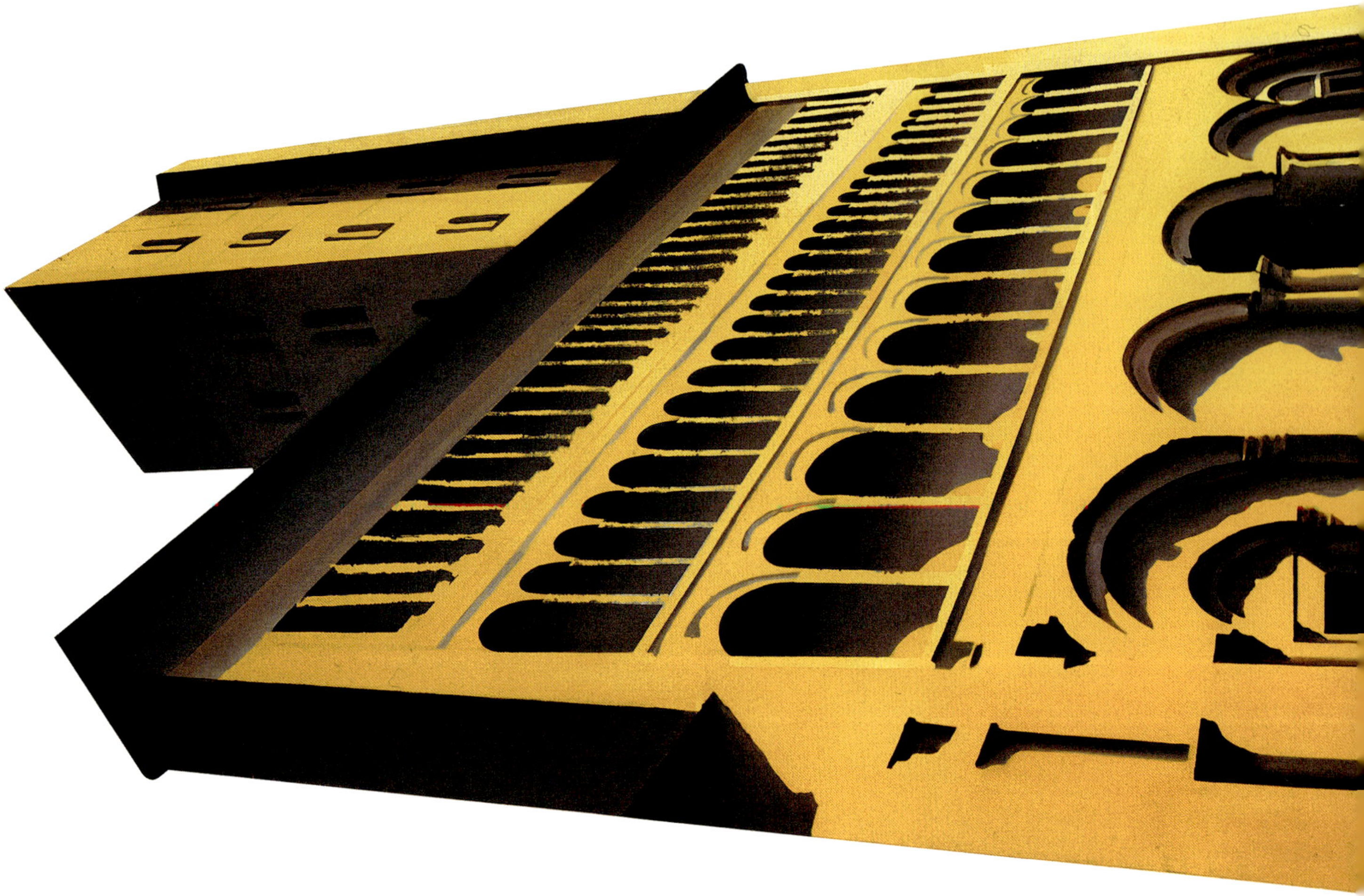

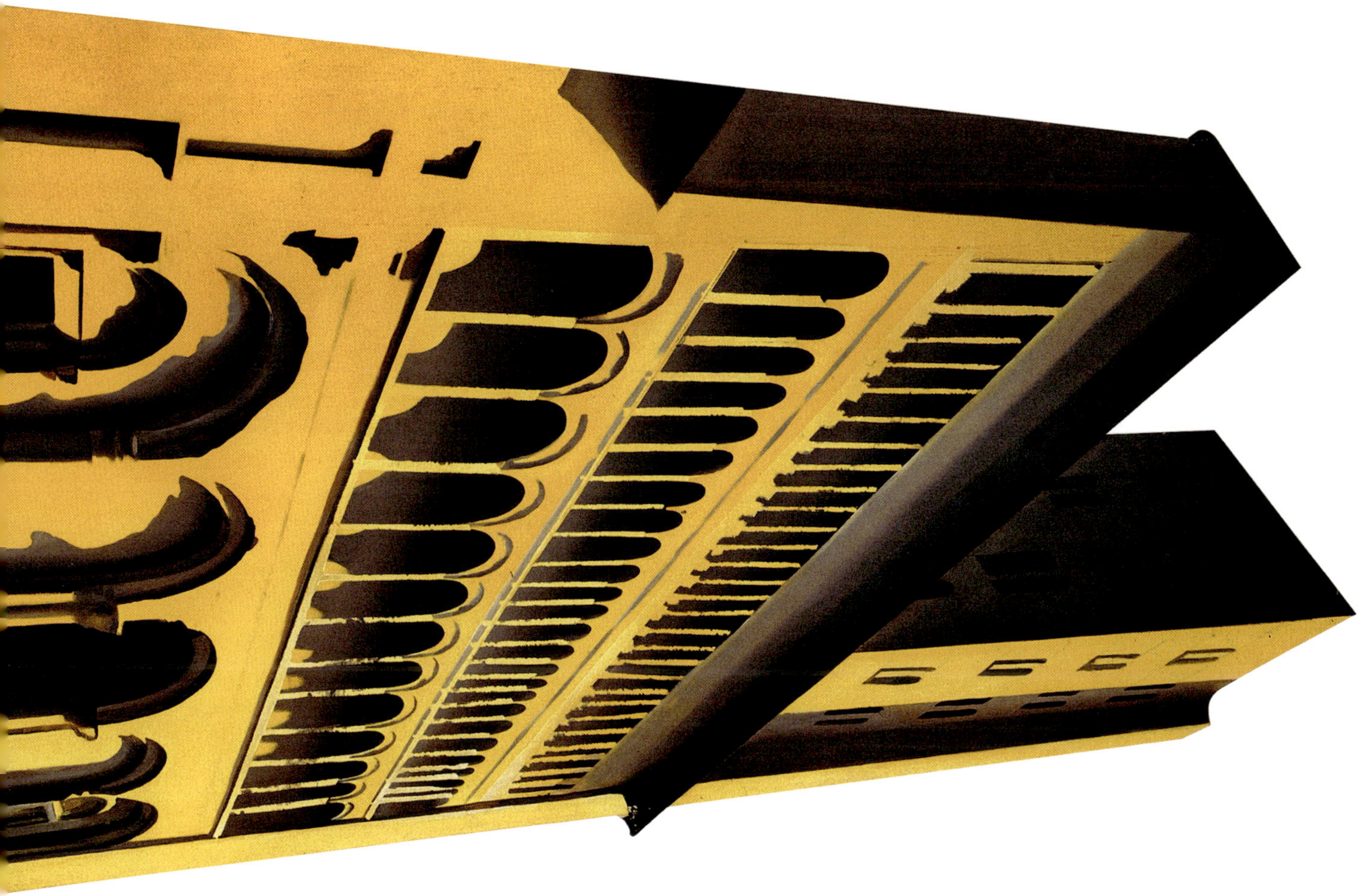

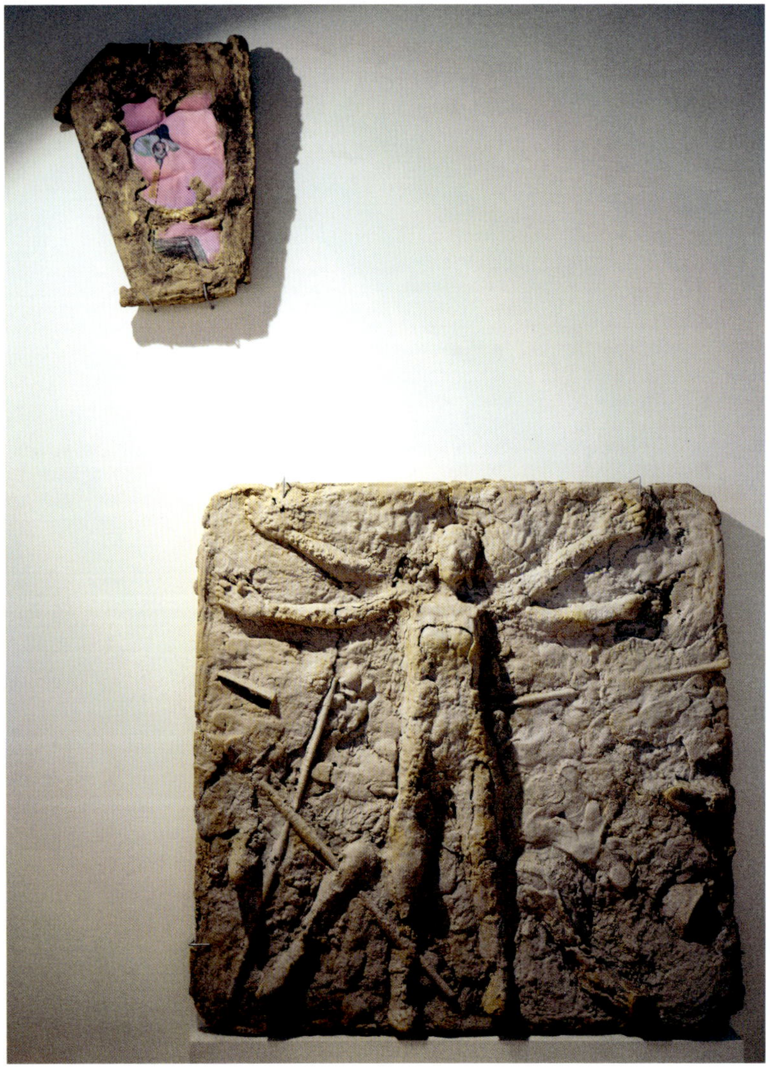

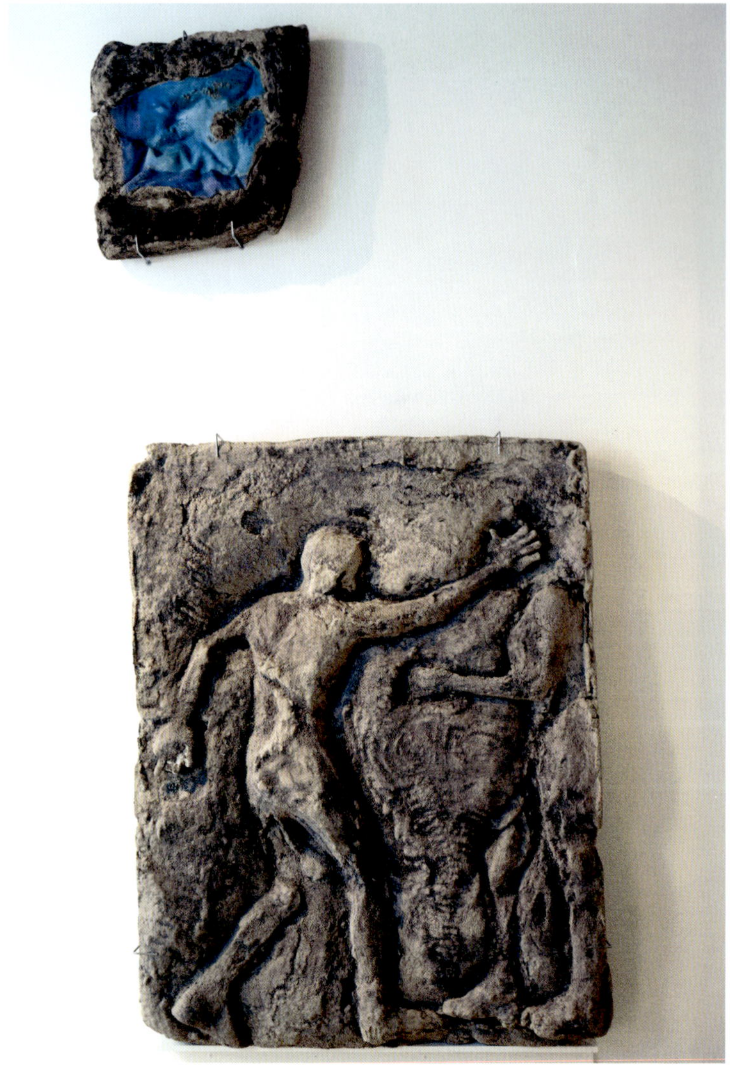

11

Momentum Mortis, 1990
Three images from the original installation at
Phyllis Kind Gallery

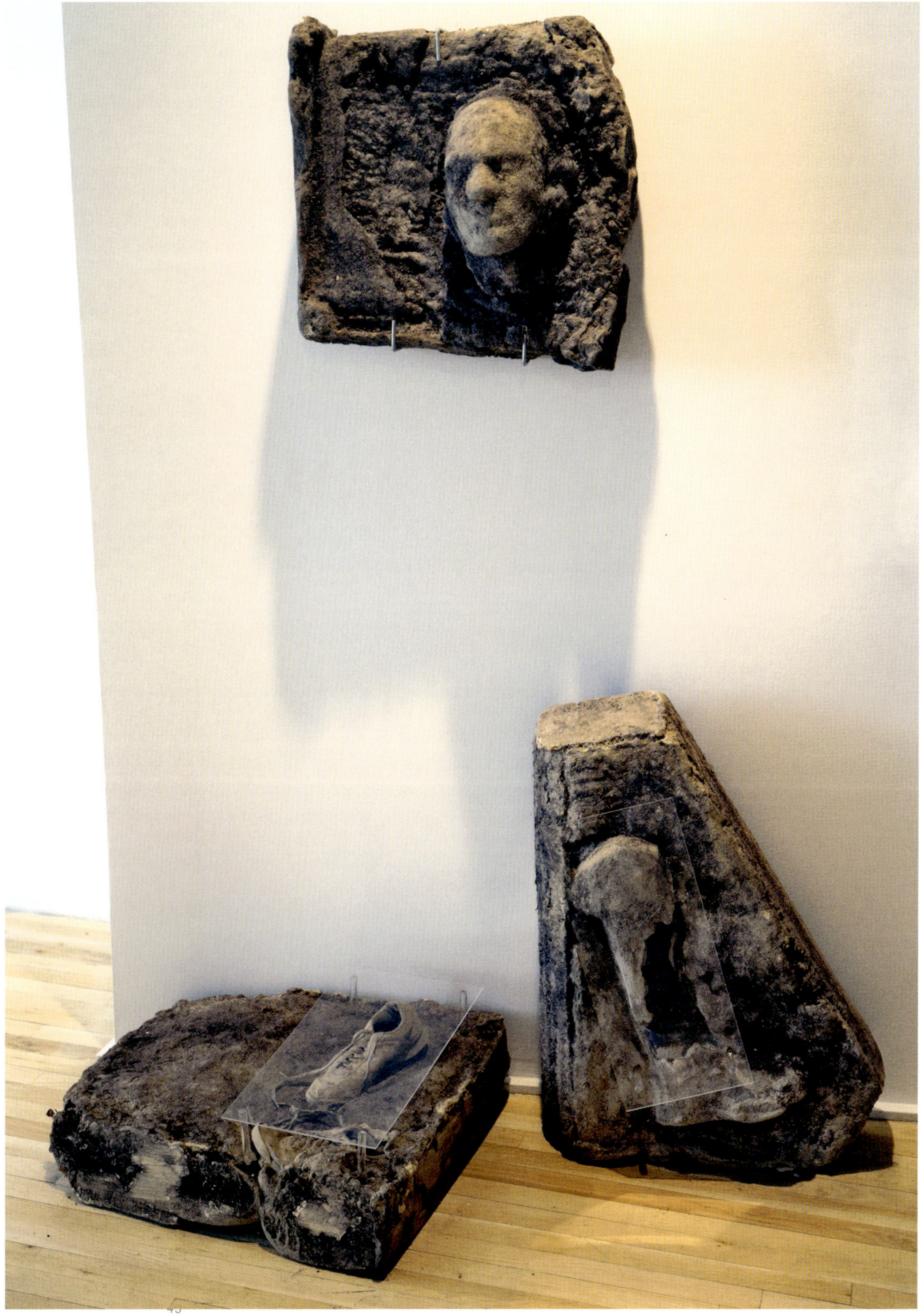

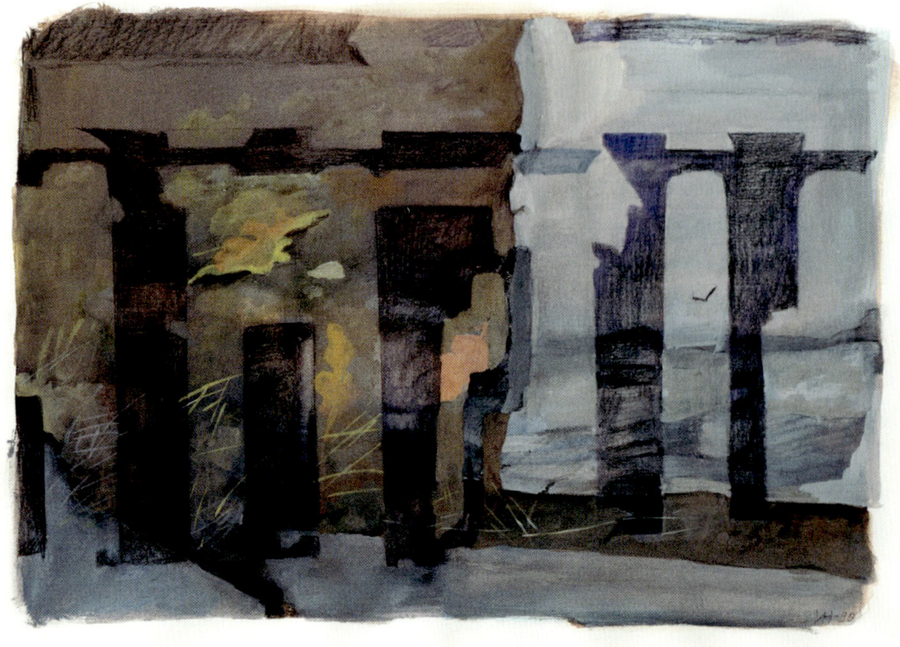

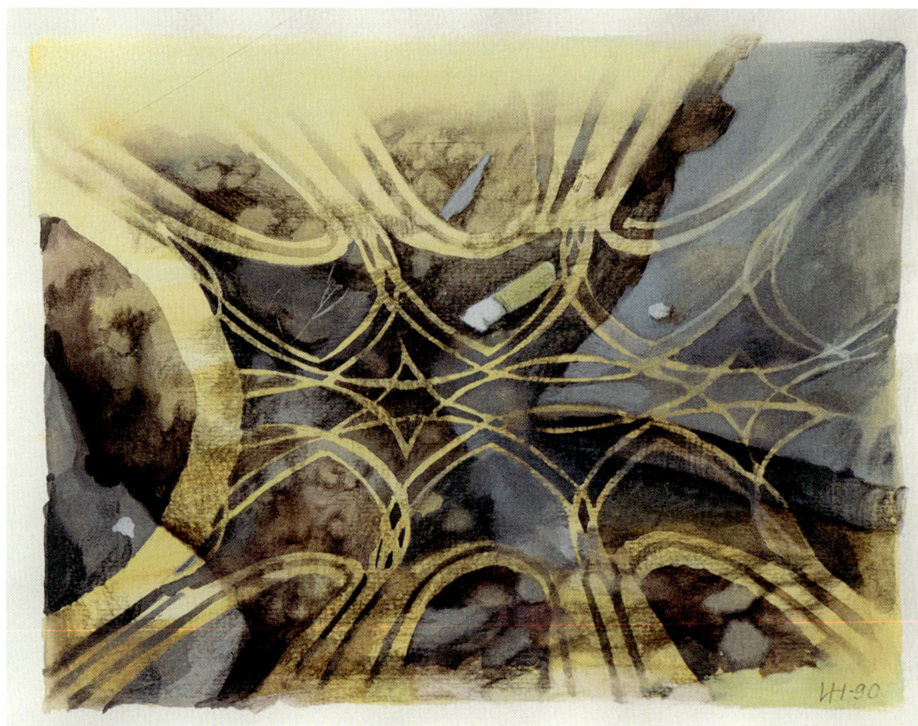

12

Untitled, 1990
Watercolor, gouache, and crayon on paper
14$\frac{1}{8}$ × 19$\frac{5}{8}$ in. (36 × 50 cm)
Gift of Vals Osborne and José Moreno-Lacalle
ZIMMERLI ART MUSEUM

13

Untitled, 1990
Watercolor and crayon on paper
13$\frac{3}{4}$ × 16$\frac{7}{8}$ in. (35 × 43 cm)
Gift of Vals Osborne and José Moreno-Lacalle
ZIMMERLI ART MUSEUM

14

Eye, 1992

Oil, acrylic, and plaster on Masonite

Panel (irregular): 31⅜ × 45¼ × 1 in. (79.7 × 115 × 2.5 cm)

Gift of Vals Osborne and José Moreno-Lacalle

ZIMMERLI ART MUSEUM

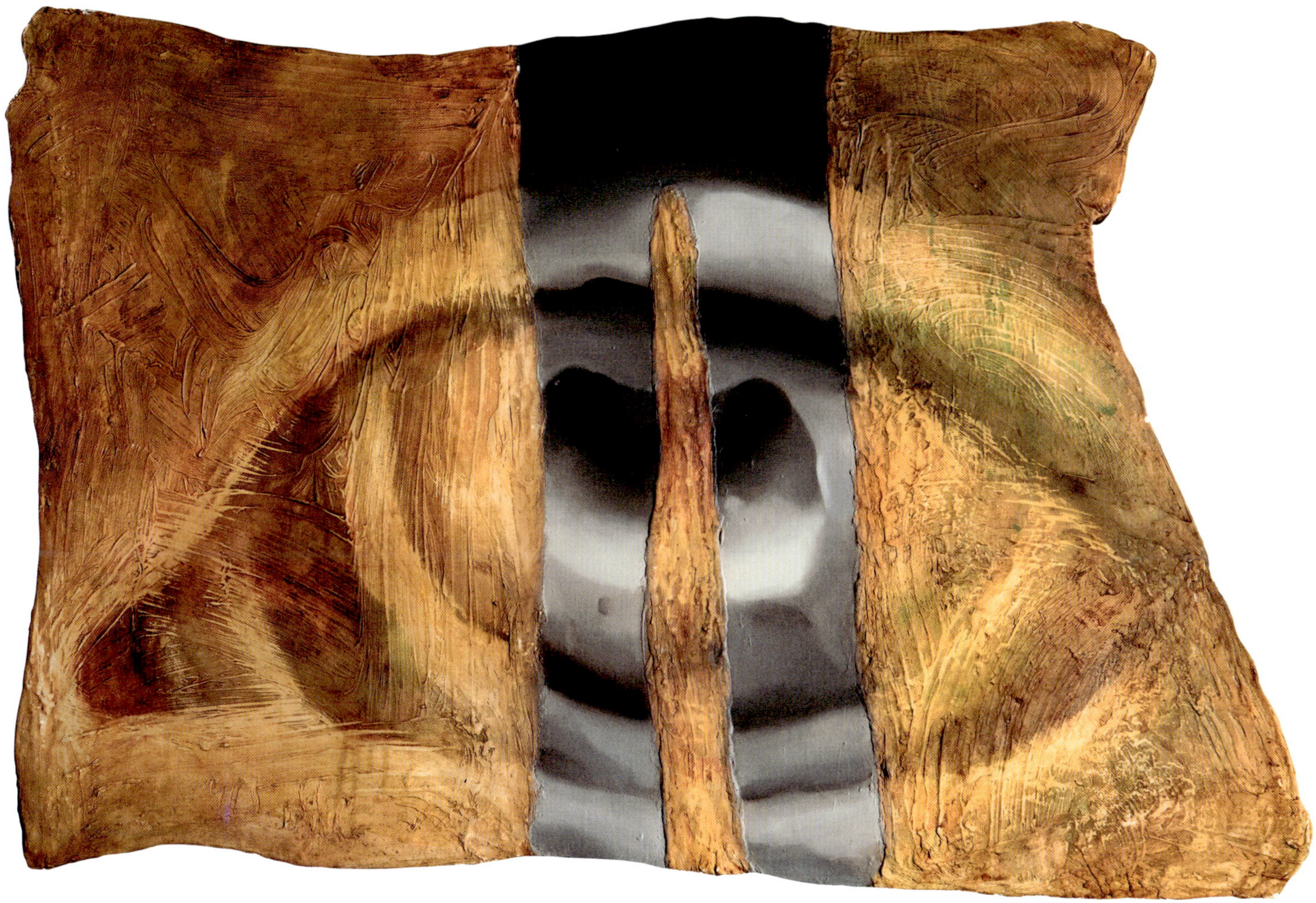

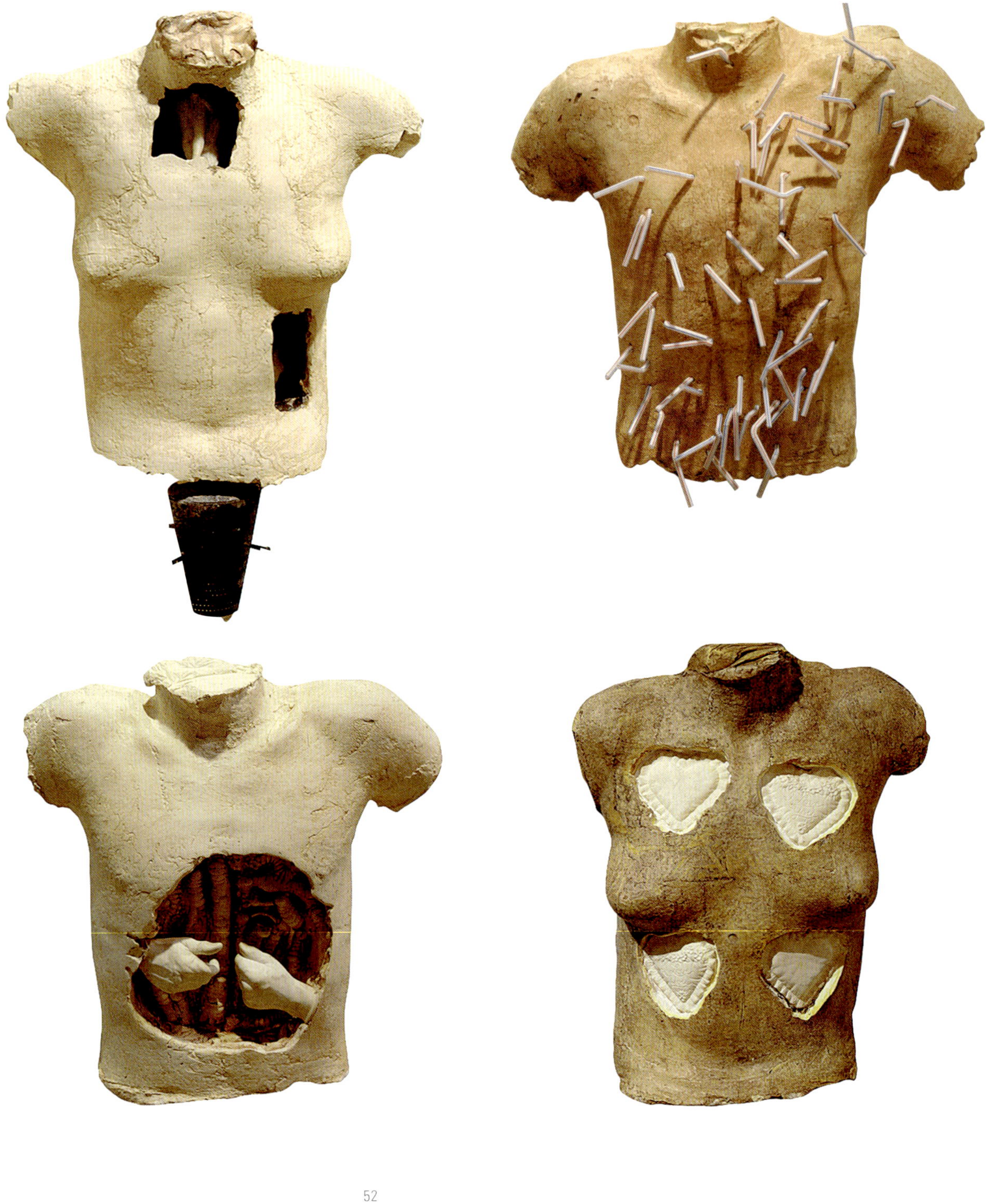

15

***Four Torsos* from the *Untitled* installation at Phyllis Kind Gallery**, 1992

Plaster and mixed media

20 × 19½ × 5½ in. (51 × 50 × 14 cm)

20½ × 16½ × 5 in. (52 × 42 × 13 cm)

27½ × 19½ × 4 in. (70 × 50 × 10 cm)

24½ × 22 × 5 in. (62 × 56 × 13 cm)

COLLECTION OF THE ARTIST

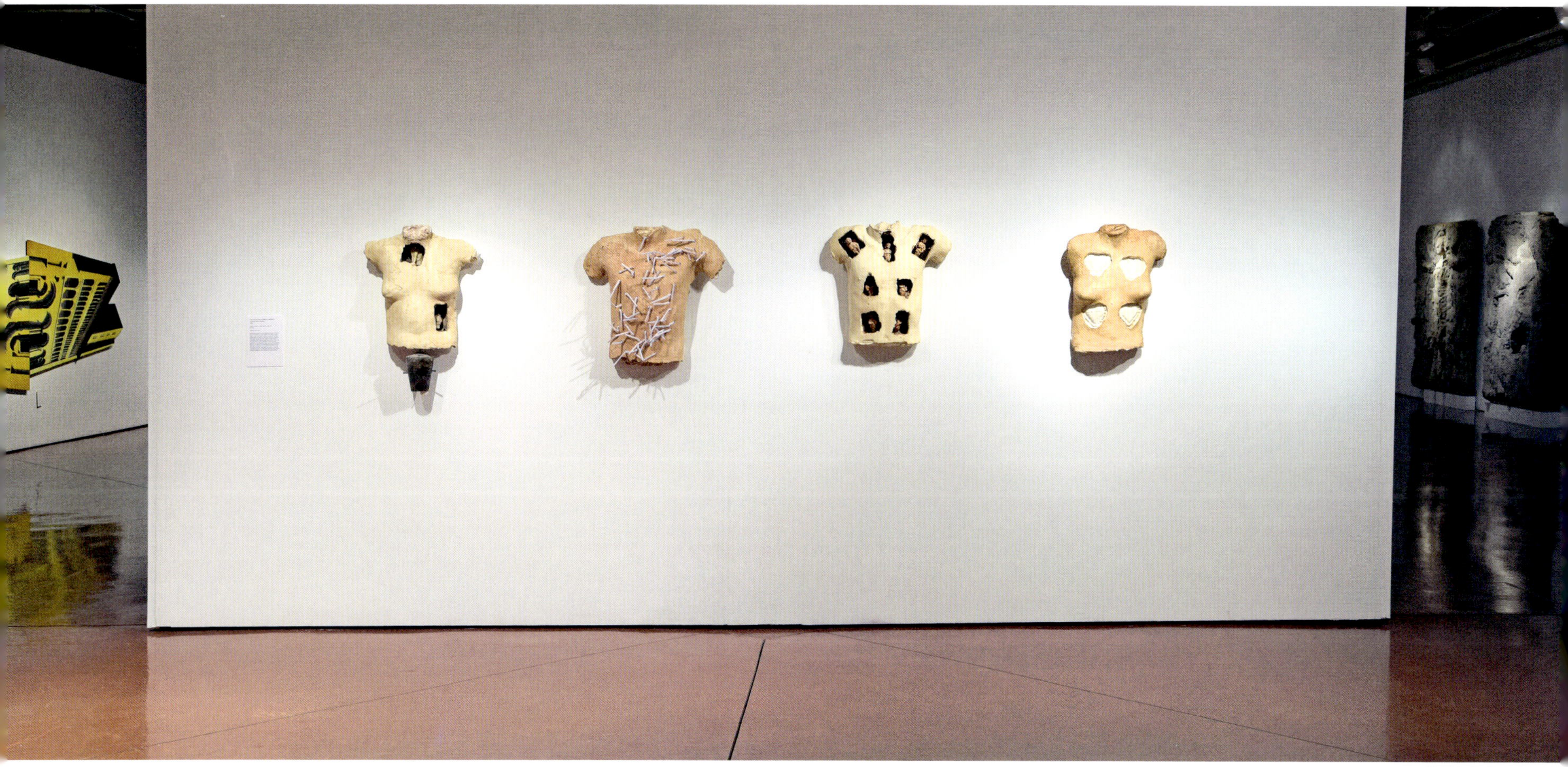

Four Torsos, 1992, installation at Zimmerli Art Museum, 2019

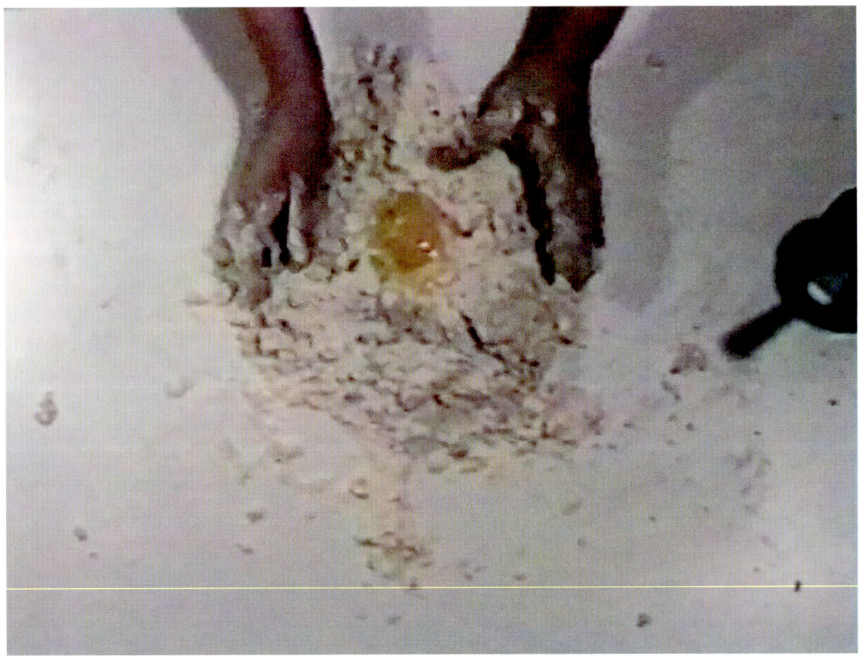

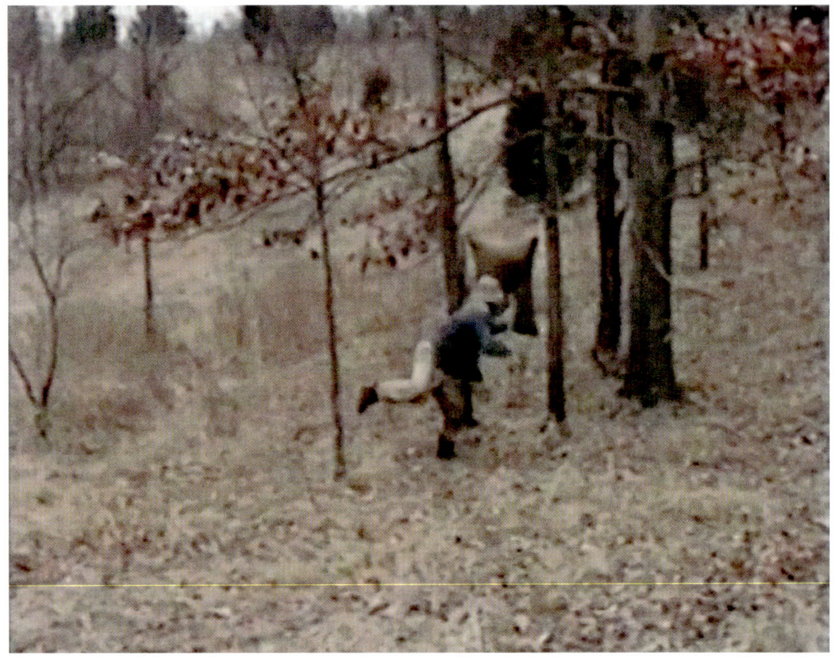

16
Queen (details from video), 1996
Video, 25:29 mins.
COLLECTION OF THE ARTIST

17
Queen, 1996
Iron, aluminum, papier-mâché, parachute silk, and wooden pedestal with electrical and electronic parts
93½ × 27 × 27 in. (238 × 69 × 69 cm) deflated
144 × 27 × 27 in. (366 × 69 × 69 cm) inflated
COLLECTION OF THE ARTIST

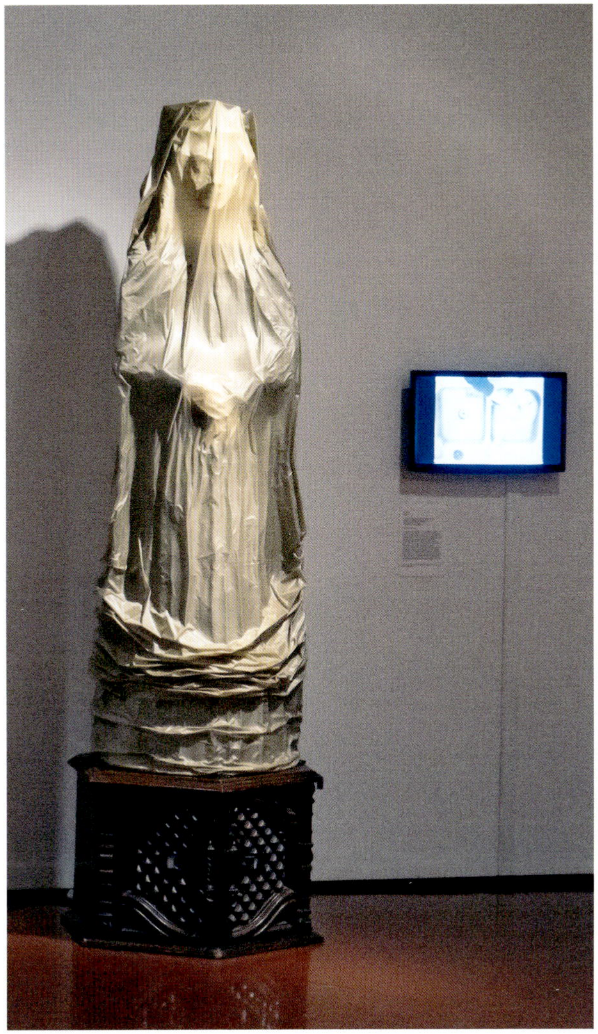

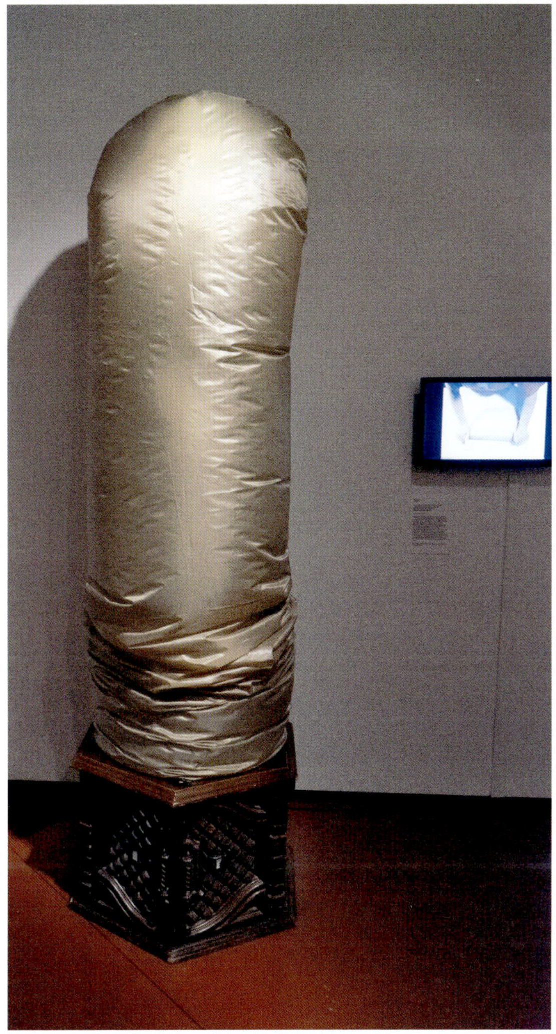

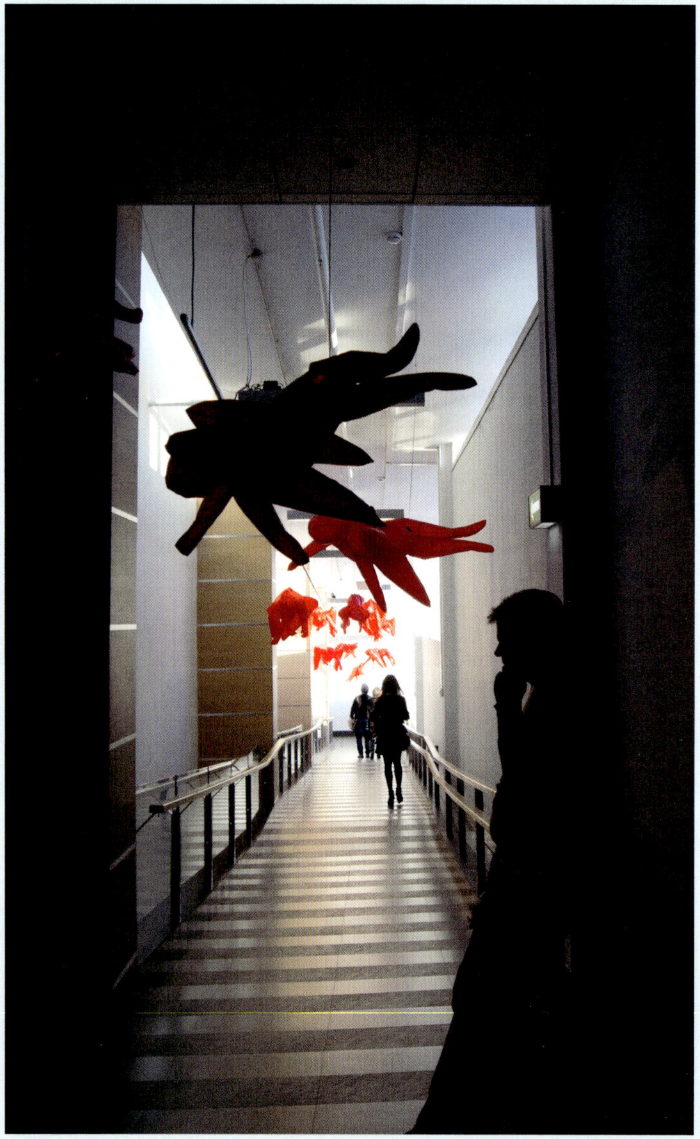

18

Annunciation: Red Angels, 2000
Installation at the Worker and Kolkhoz Woman Center, Moscow

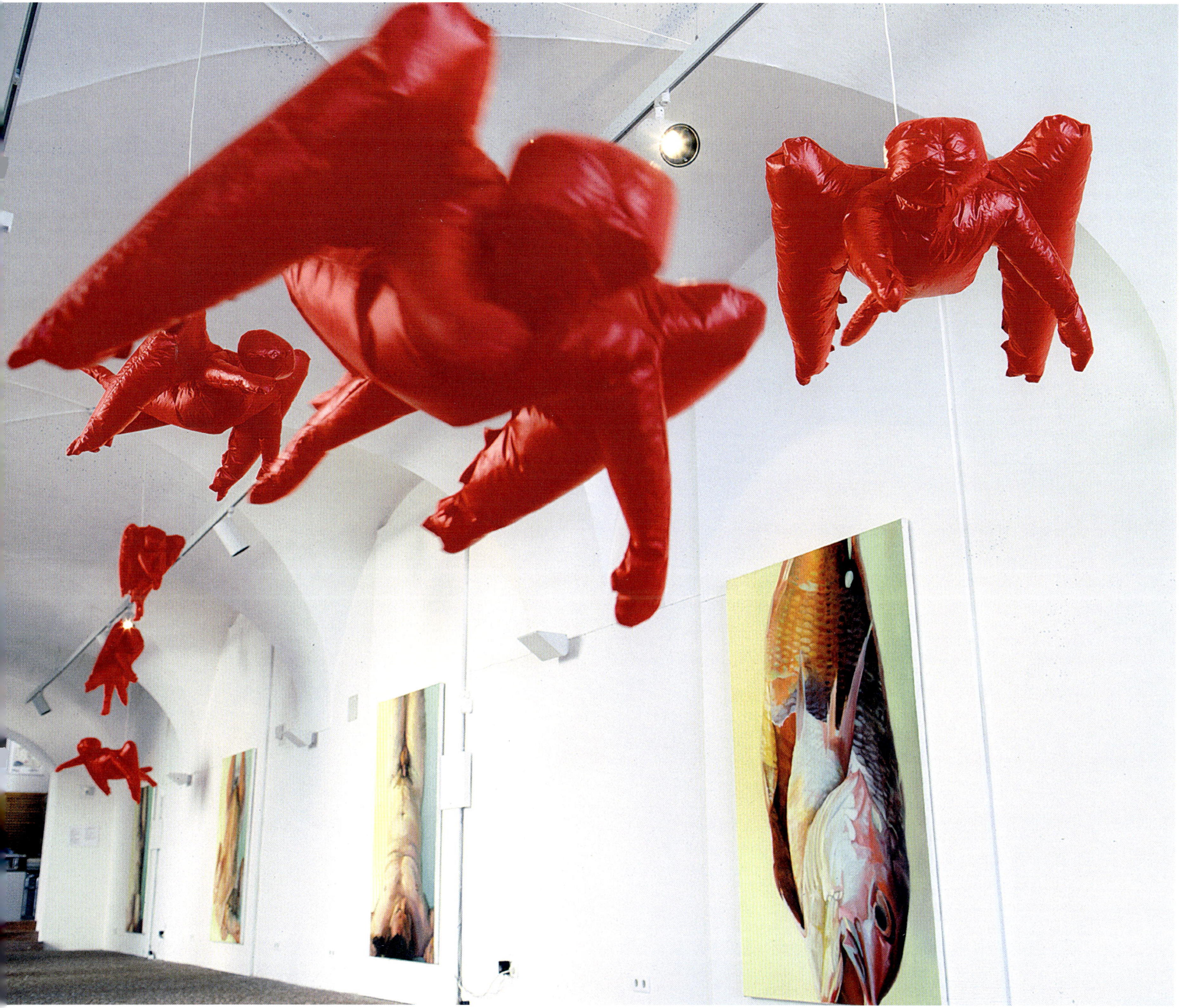

19
Skin No. 1, 2010
Inkjet print on latex
30½ × 21½ in. (77 × 54 cm)
COLLECTION OF THE ARTIST

20
Skin No. 3, 2010
Inkjet print on latex
33 × 28 in. (85 × 69 cm)
COLLECTION OF THE ARTIST

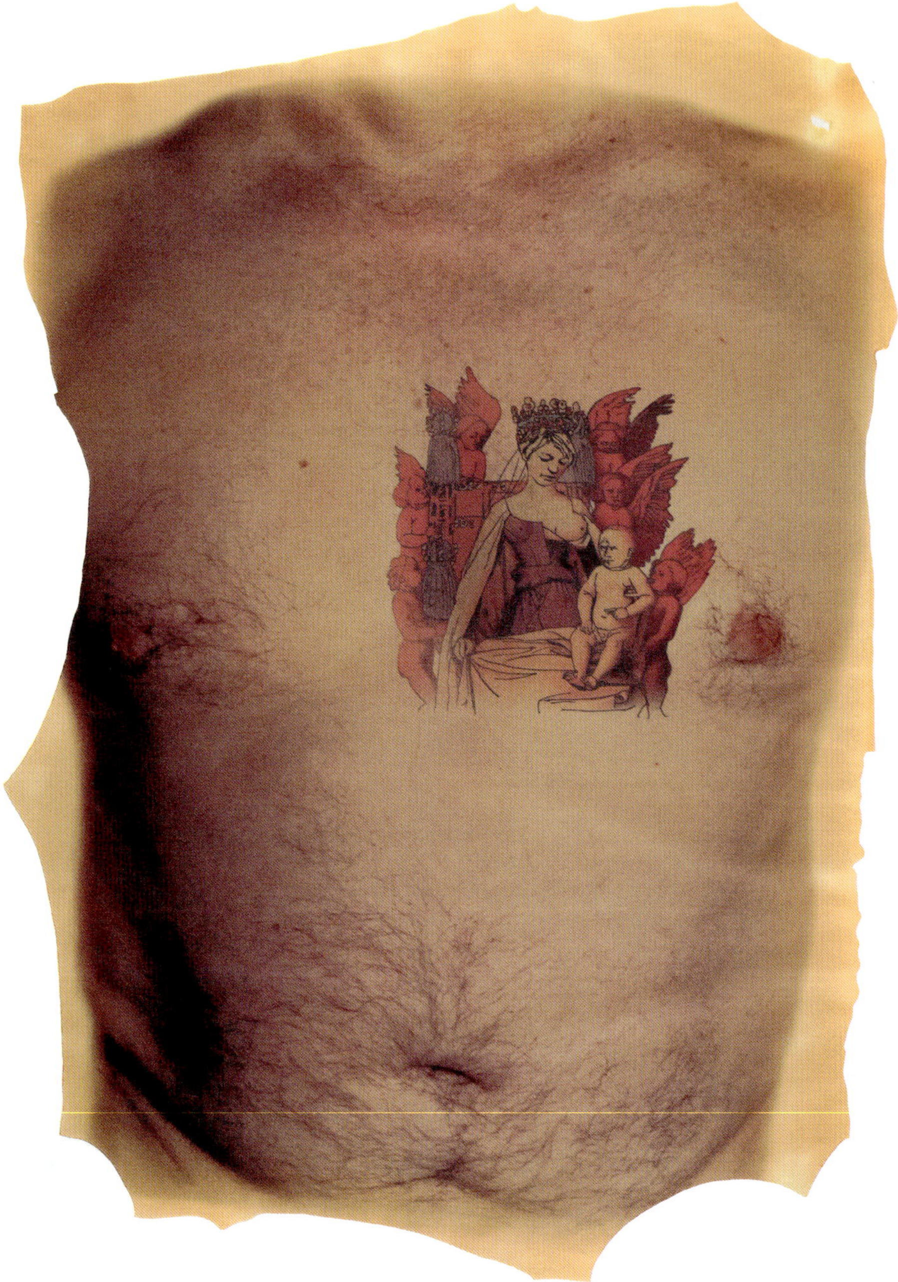

Skin No. 1 An Irish-Catholic boy named Timmy had a strict upbringing. He always said the Our Father before and after dinner. At the age of fourteen, he decided to get a tattoo of the Virgin Mary on the left side of his chest, close to his heart. At the age of eighteen, as a conscientious warrior on terror, he joined the Army and went to Iraq. On the third day there, on his way to the privy, he was accidentally shot by a fellow private, who was target-shooting lizards in his spare time. Timmy was skinned right away so his tattoo could be preserved for the Military Pride Museum in Washington, D.C., where you can view it on display from 10 a.m. to 6 p.m. on Tuesdays through Sundays; the museum is closed on Mondays. Donations are welcome.

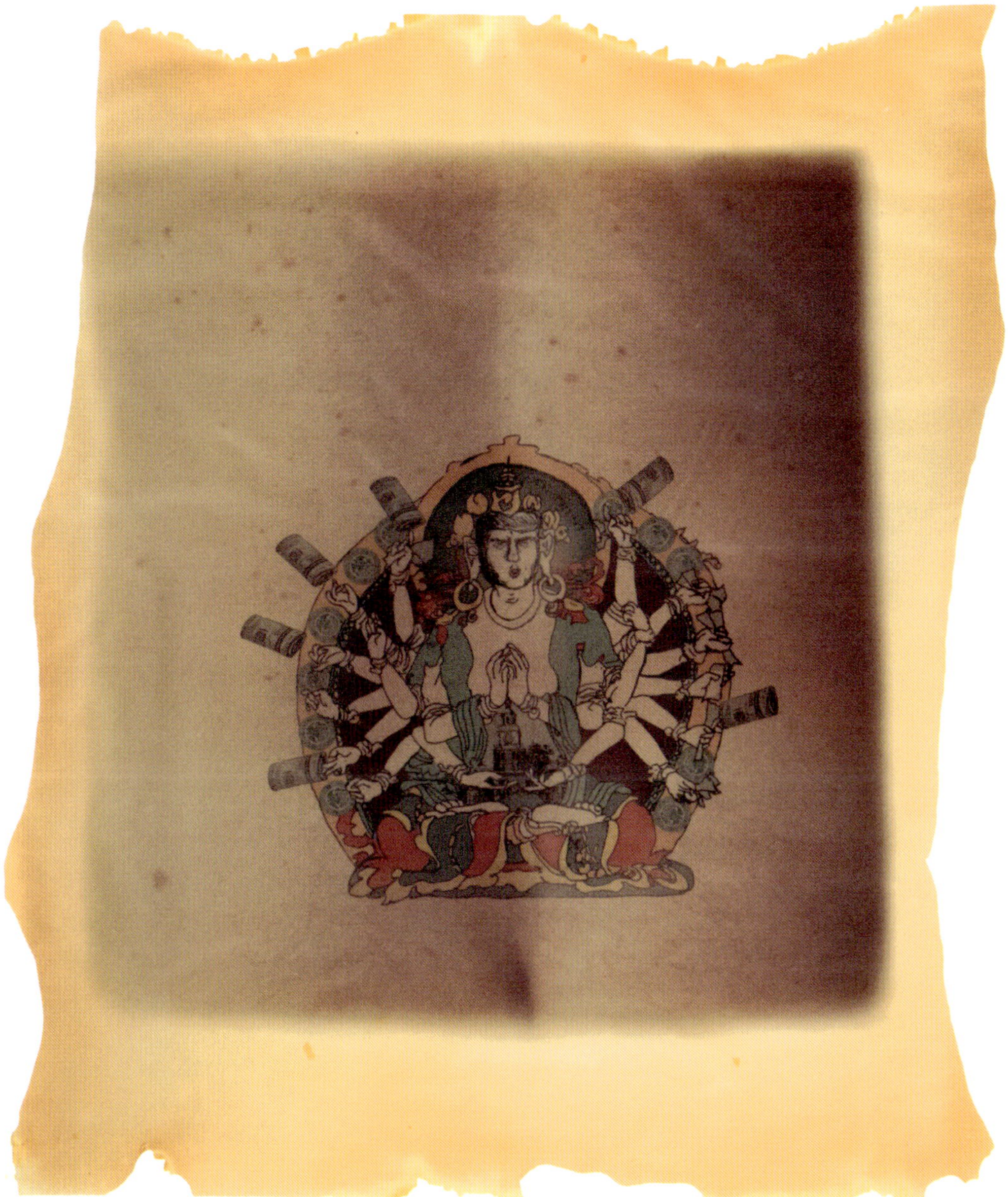

Skin No. 3 Badri was born to a poor Buddhist family in Mumbai, India. He succeeded in math and computing at the local school. His dream was to become a Wall Street broker and bring wealth to his family. After winning a national English spelling bee competition, he met Cindy McGraw, who decided to bring him home with her to America. In New York, he obtained a tattoo of Buddha with dollar bills in all of his hands, for good fortune. After graduating from Princeton Law School, he became a broker on Wall Street. One weekend, he went quail hunting at a ranch owned by a friend of his adoptive parents. One of the senators present mistakenly shot him right beneath the twelfth vertebra. Badri was properly skinned; the Buddha hide hangs above the fireplace, in the dining room of the McGraw residence. You can view it on Cindy's website, at www.cindy.gov.

21
Skin No. 4, 2010
Inkjet print on latex
22 × 24½ in. (55 × 62 cm)
COLLECTION OF THE ARTIST

22
Skin No. 5, 2010
Inkjet print on latex
35 × 25 in. (89 × 64 cm)
COLLECTION OF THE ARTIST

23
Skin No. 10, 2010
Inkjet print on latex
27½ × 26 in. (71 × 66 cm)
COLLECTION OF THE ARTIST

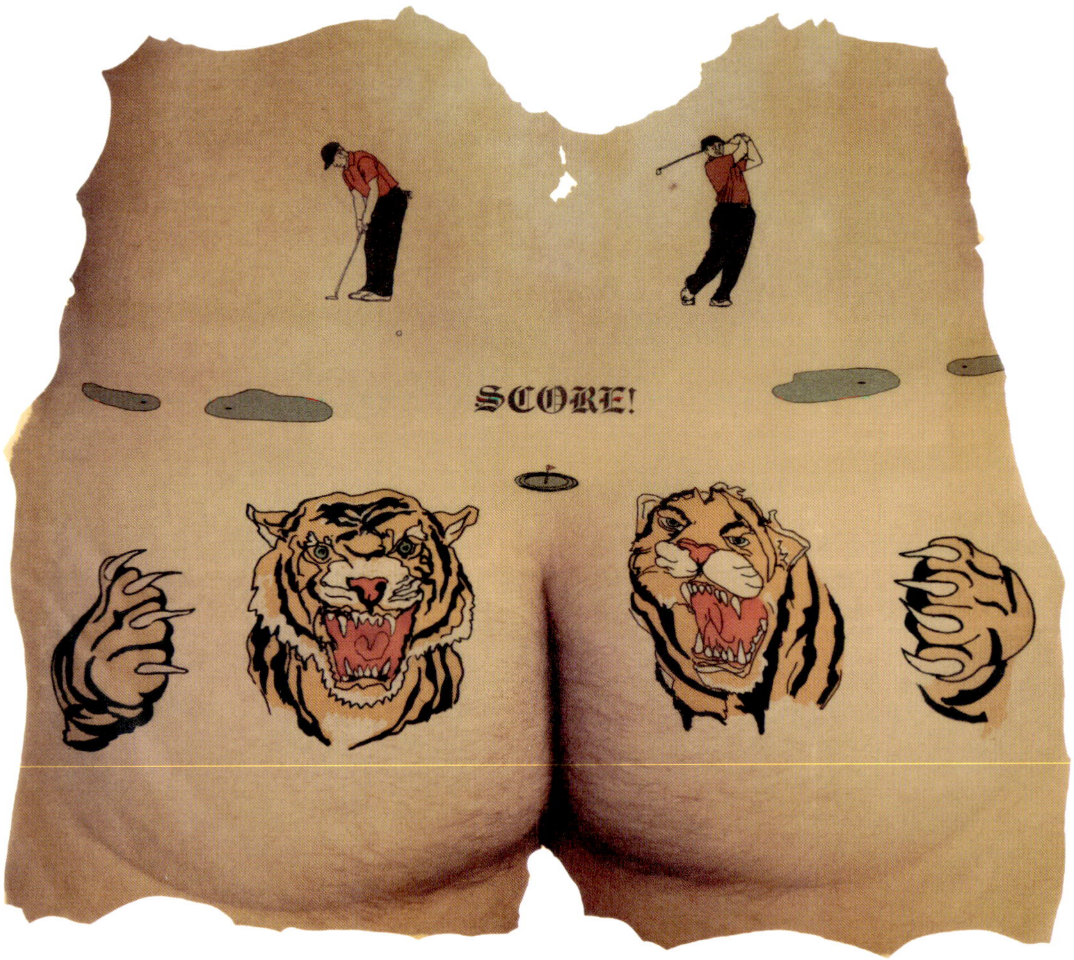

Skin No. 4 Brooke was born in Australia, the daughter of well-known tiger poachers. For initiation rites, images of tigers were inscribed on her back and cheeks. Instilled with a love of risky adventure since early childhood, she became the champion of the World Poker Tour 2012, raking in 400 million dollars. As a result, her heart opened to God, and she decided to donate a quarter of her winnings to a worthy cause. She went to the Gaza Strip to write a check to the Israeli-Palestinian Young People's Equal Rights Brigade. Unfortunately, she and her bodyguards were suffocated at the Shalom Hotel. Her well-known tattooed hide surfaced on a video originally broadcast by Al Jazeera. In the video, Donald Trump warns youth not to donate gambling money to holy causes, using Brooke as an example. The speech had over a million hits on You Tube, at http://www.youtube.com /watch?v=xGZaCnfNgLE.

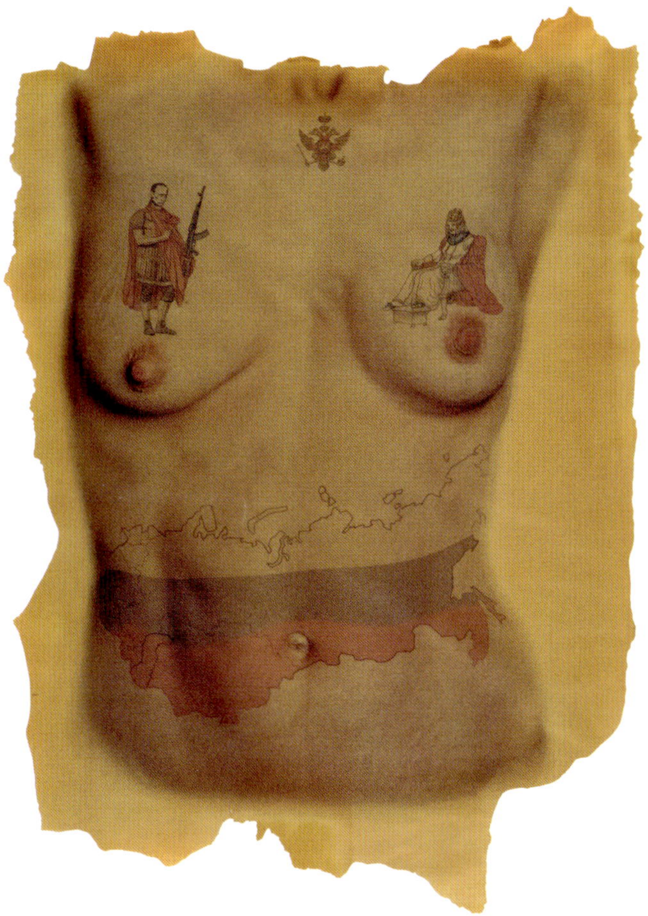

Skin No. 5 Nadezda came from a large family in a small town in central Russia. She wanted a different life for herself, and took a chance in the big city of Moscow. She didn't want to become a prostitute, and from her fellow girls living in Moscow's central train station, she learned that a prosperous gallery owner wanted to become a famous artist himself, and was hiring people for a thousand dollars only to be tattooed and videoed for his first art project. She was lucky to get the job. Unfortunately, later that day, she was slain by a homeless girl from Kazan. Rumour has it that the girl and a junkie from Lubertzi took Nadezda's money and ran to Crimea to spare themselves the cold Moscow winter. Her former friends near the train station amateurishly skinned her and sold her trimmings to an emerging artist for five hundred dollars. Her skin can be viewed at the artist's next exhibit at Access Gallery Foundation, by appointment only.

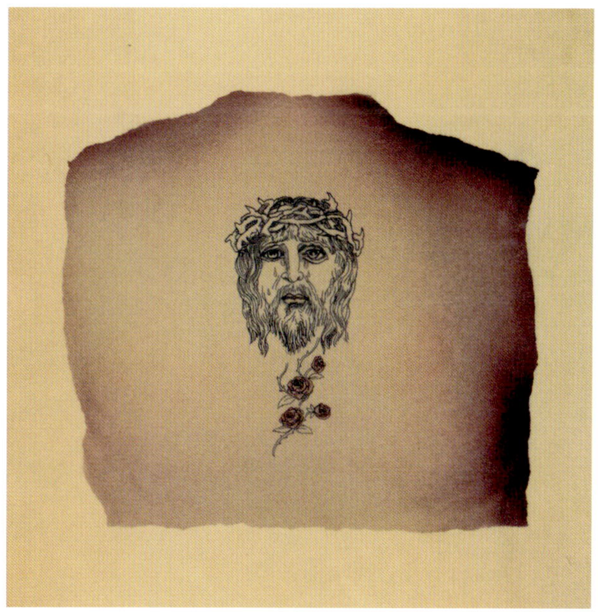

Skin No. 10 Alison was an ambitious young woman from Middletown, Missouri. In order to pay for her medical education (she wanted to become a dentist) she went to a military academy in Fort Wayne, Texas. While being given a medical assessment, she was shot by a disturbed staff psychiatrist. She had just gotten a tattoo as a gift from her parents for her eighteenth birthday. Her mom and dad had tattooed her themselves, taking turns in their garden toolshed. While inflicting minor pain on their daughter, they experienced unprecedented orgasmic thrills. 'As a dentist, you should know pain,' they explained. She was prepared, and her skin became Exhibit # 1841 in the prosecution's case against the psychiatrist. On 12 December, you can view this homemade, yet inspiring tattoo for one time only at the Military Court Building in Fort Bluff, Virginia.

24

Gaze, 2016
Video, 8:00 mins.
Based on the work by
Rembrandt, *Portrait of an Old Woman*, 1650–55,
from the Pushkin State Museum of Fine Arts, Moscow
COLLECTION OF THE ARTIST

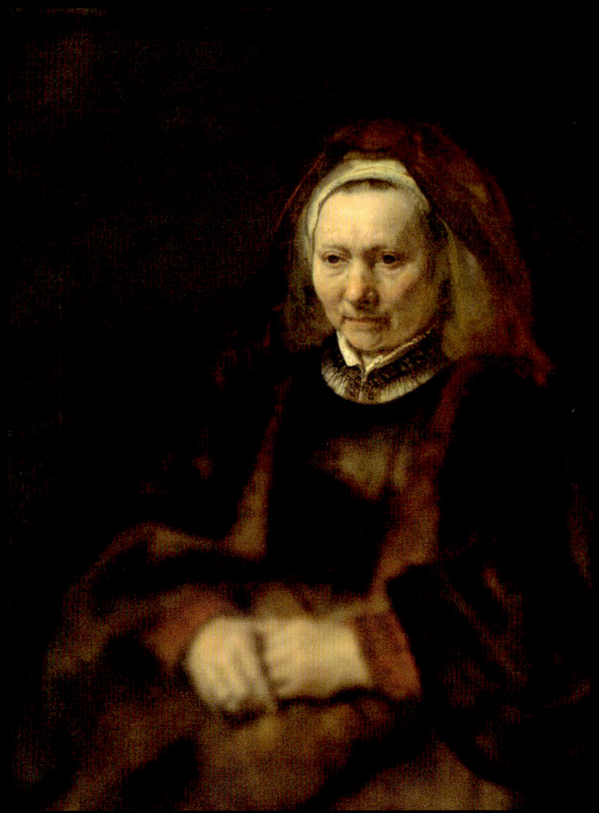

25

Gaze, 2016
Video, 7:41 mins.
Based on the work by François Boucher,
Hercules and Omphale, 1732–34,
from the Pushkin State Museum of
Fine Arts, Moscow
COLLECTION OF THE ARTIST

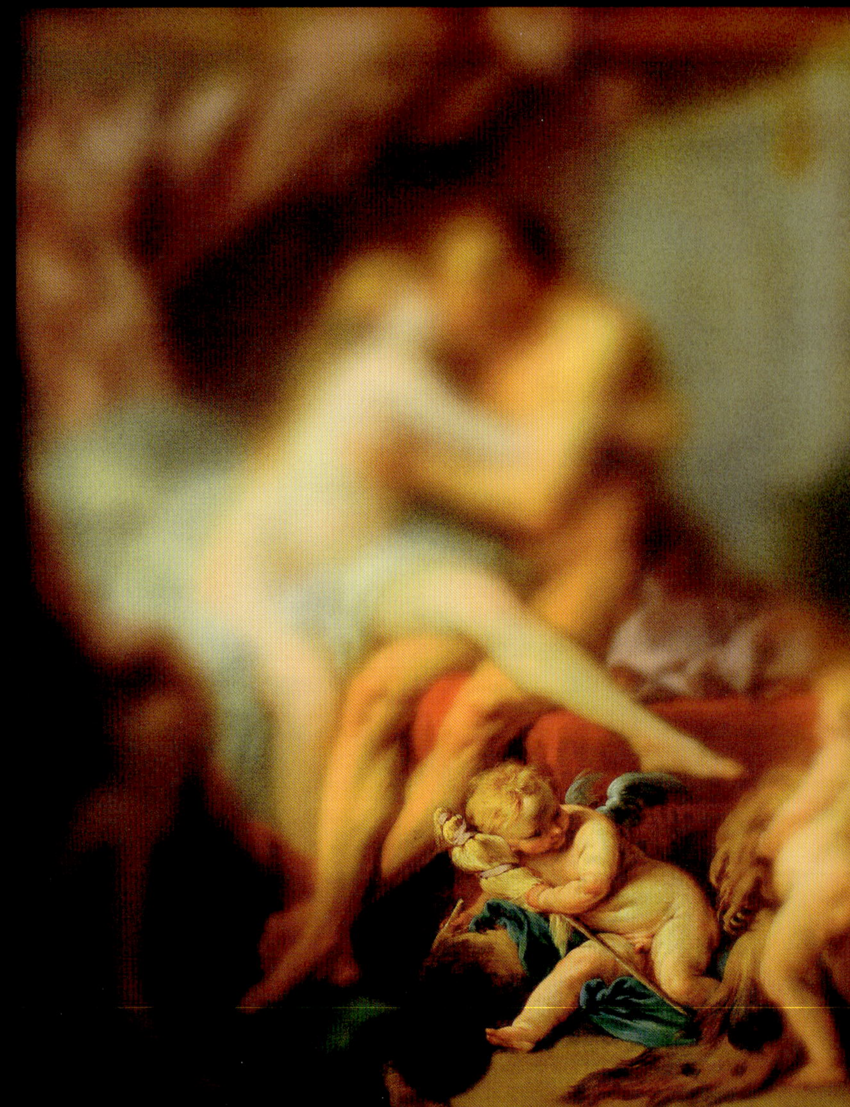

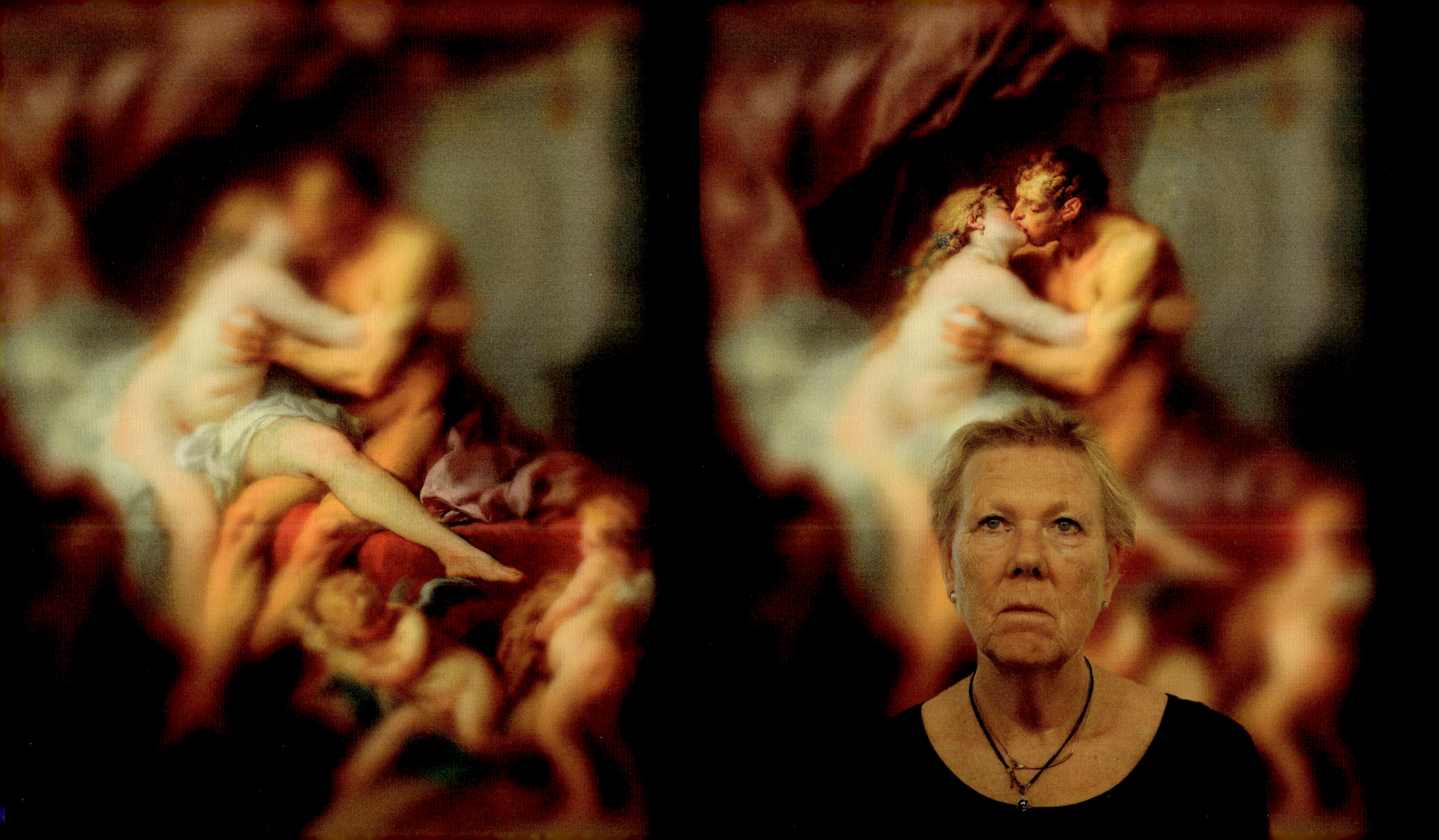

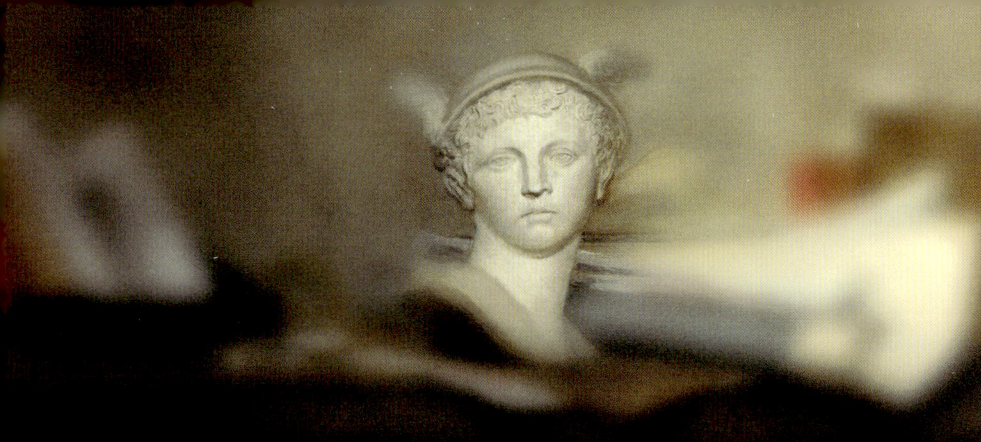

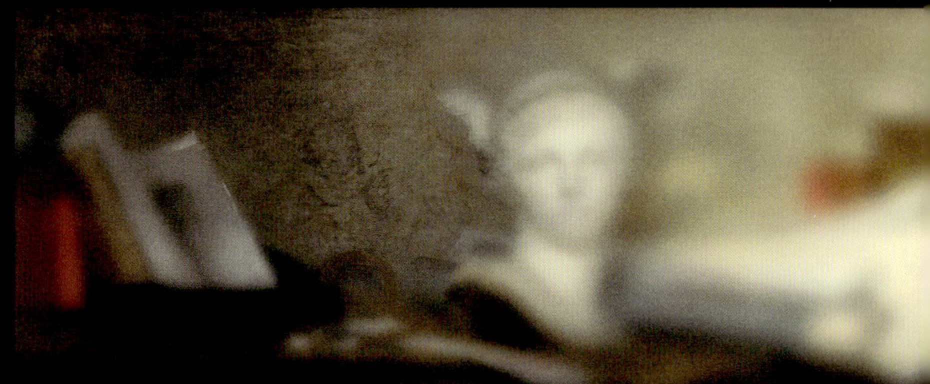

26

Gaze, 2016
Video, 3:34 mins.
Based on the work by Jean-Baptiste-Siméon Chardin,
Still Life with Attributes of the Arts, c. 1724–28,
from the Pushkin State Museum of Fine Arts, Moscow
COLLECTION OF THE ARTIST

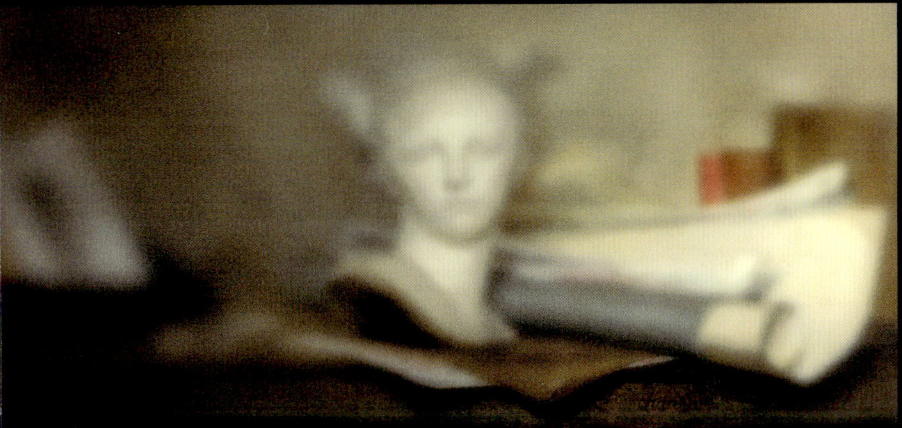

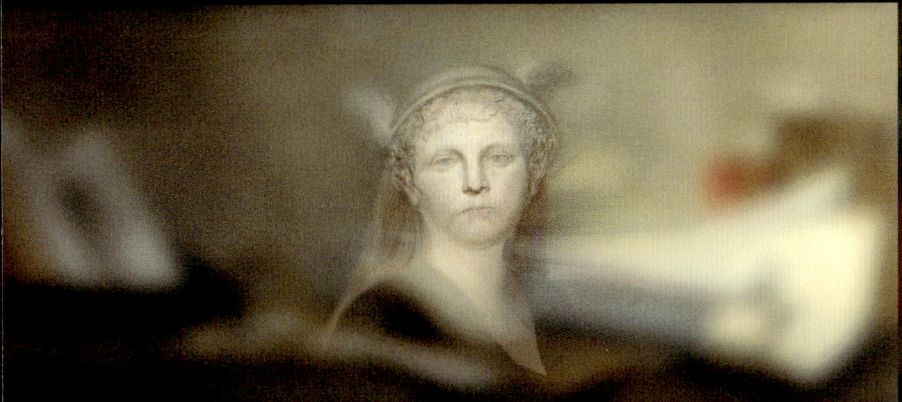

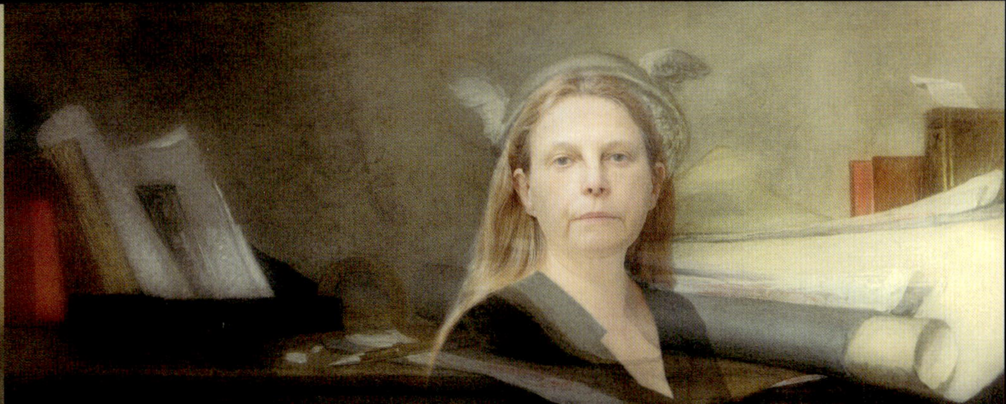

27

Gaze, 2019
Video, 7:06 mins.
Based on the work by an unidentified French artist, *Portrait of an Artist in Her Studio*, c. 1790, from the Zimmerli Art Museum
COLLECTION OF THE ARTIST

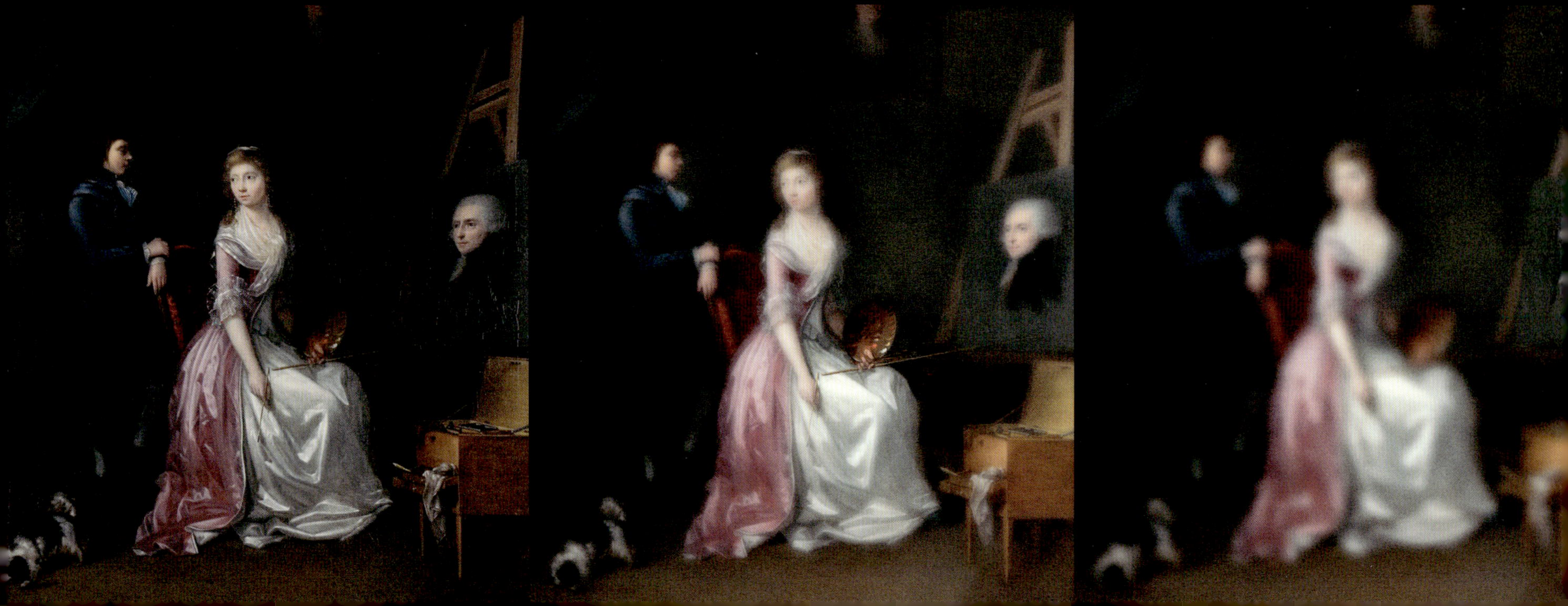

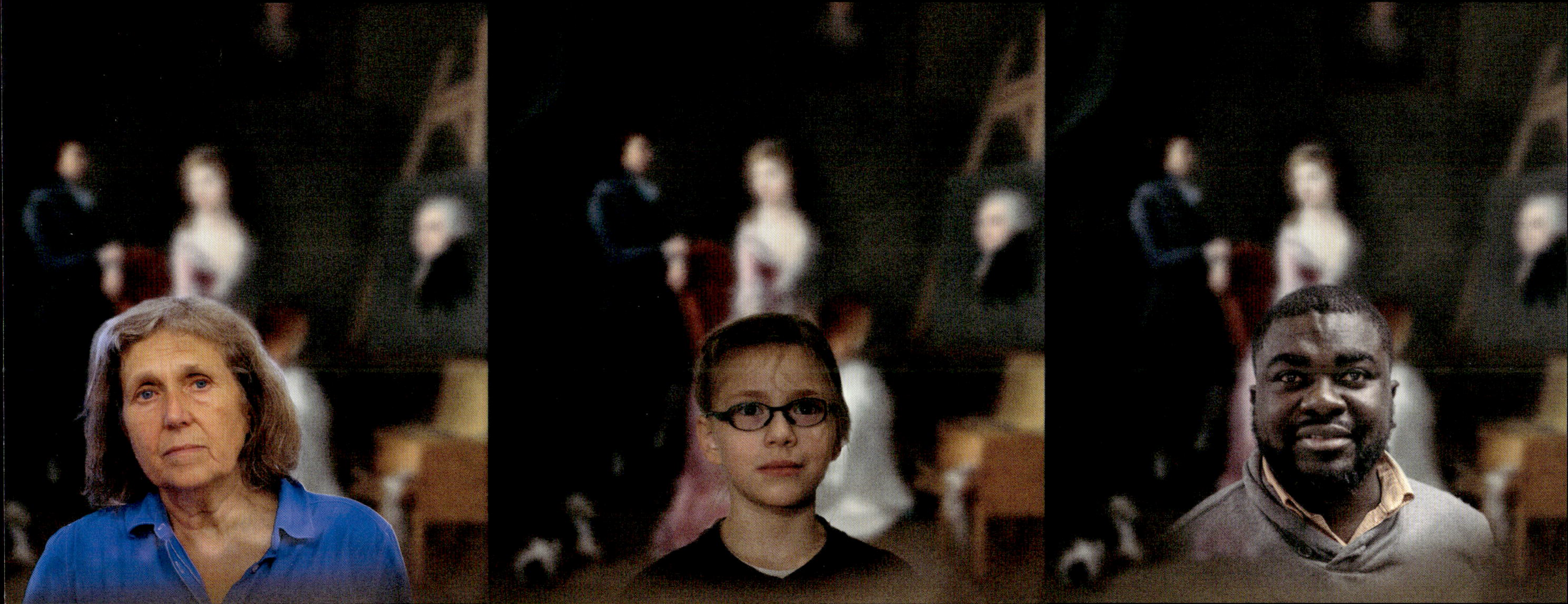

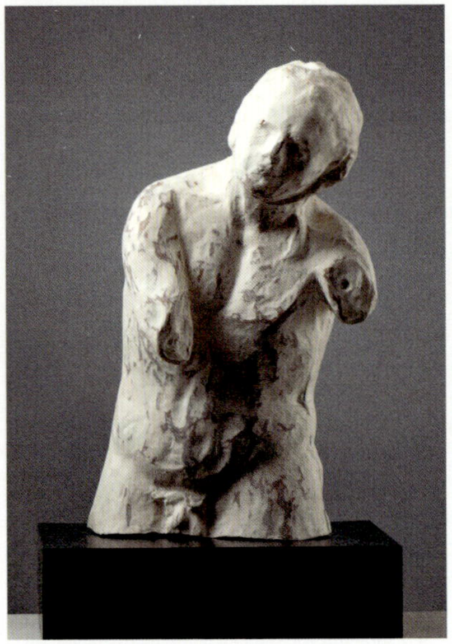

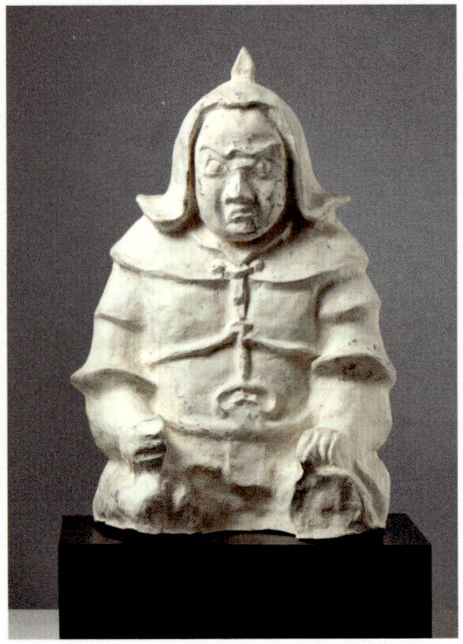

28

Battle of the Invalids, 2017, two of ten figures
Papier-mâché, UltraBoard, radio-controlled cars
Each: 27 × 16 × 16 in. (69 × 40 × 40 cm)
COLLECTION OF THE ARTIST

Below:
Battle of the Invalids, 2017
From the video projection, 28:35 mins.

Right:
Battle of the Invalids, 2017
Installation at pop/off/art gallery, Moscow
PHOTOGRAPHS COURTESY OF POP/OFF/ART GALLERY

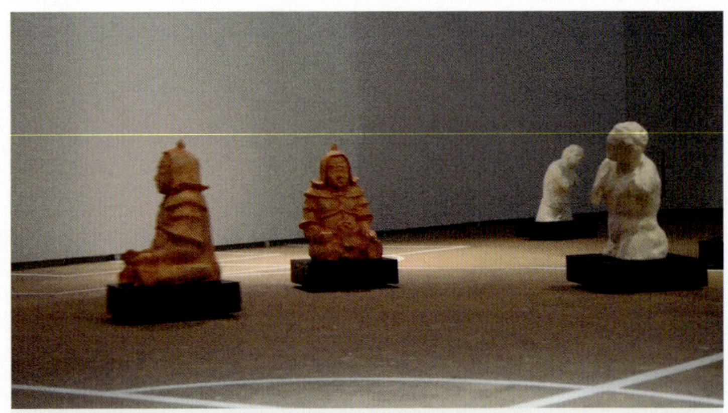

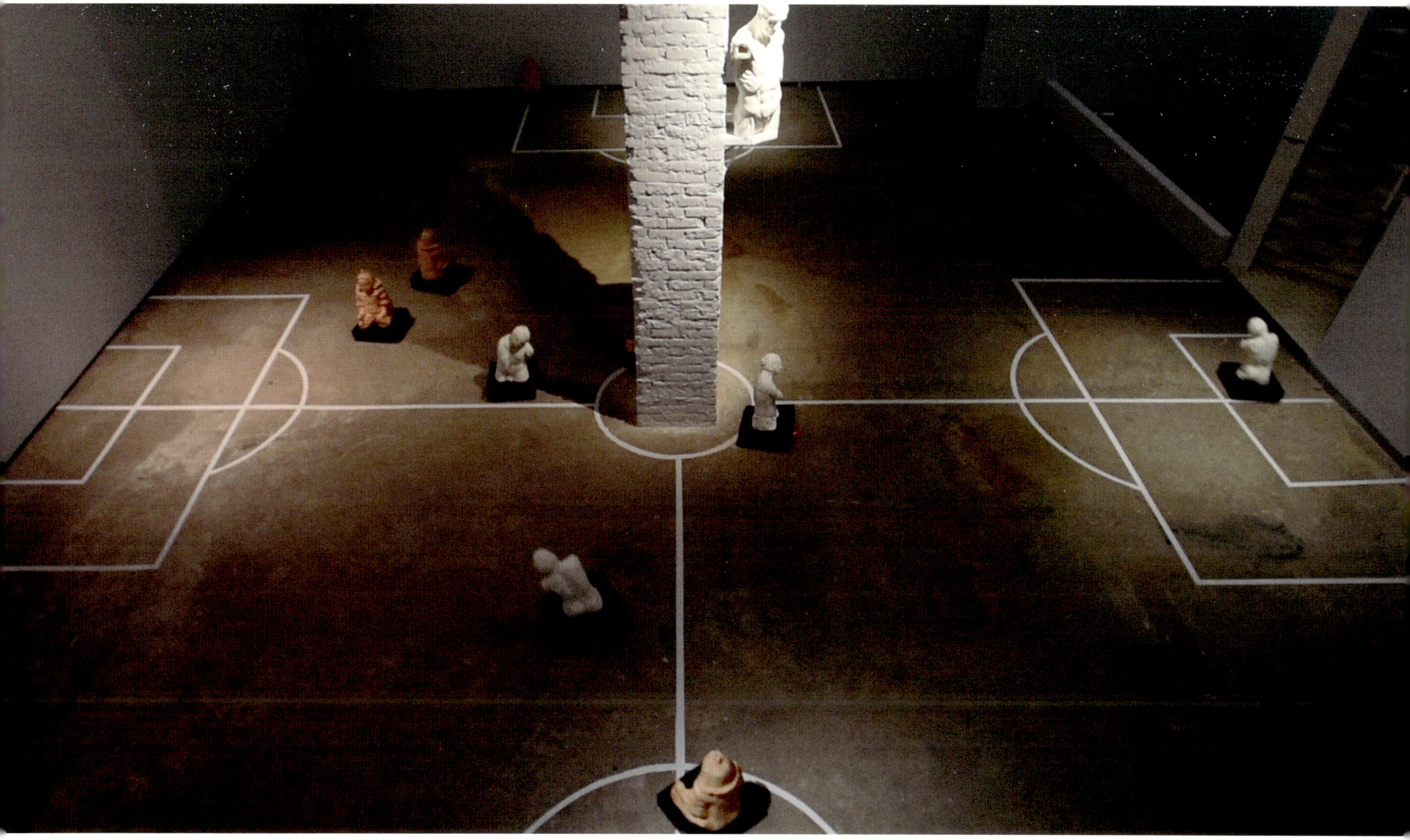

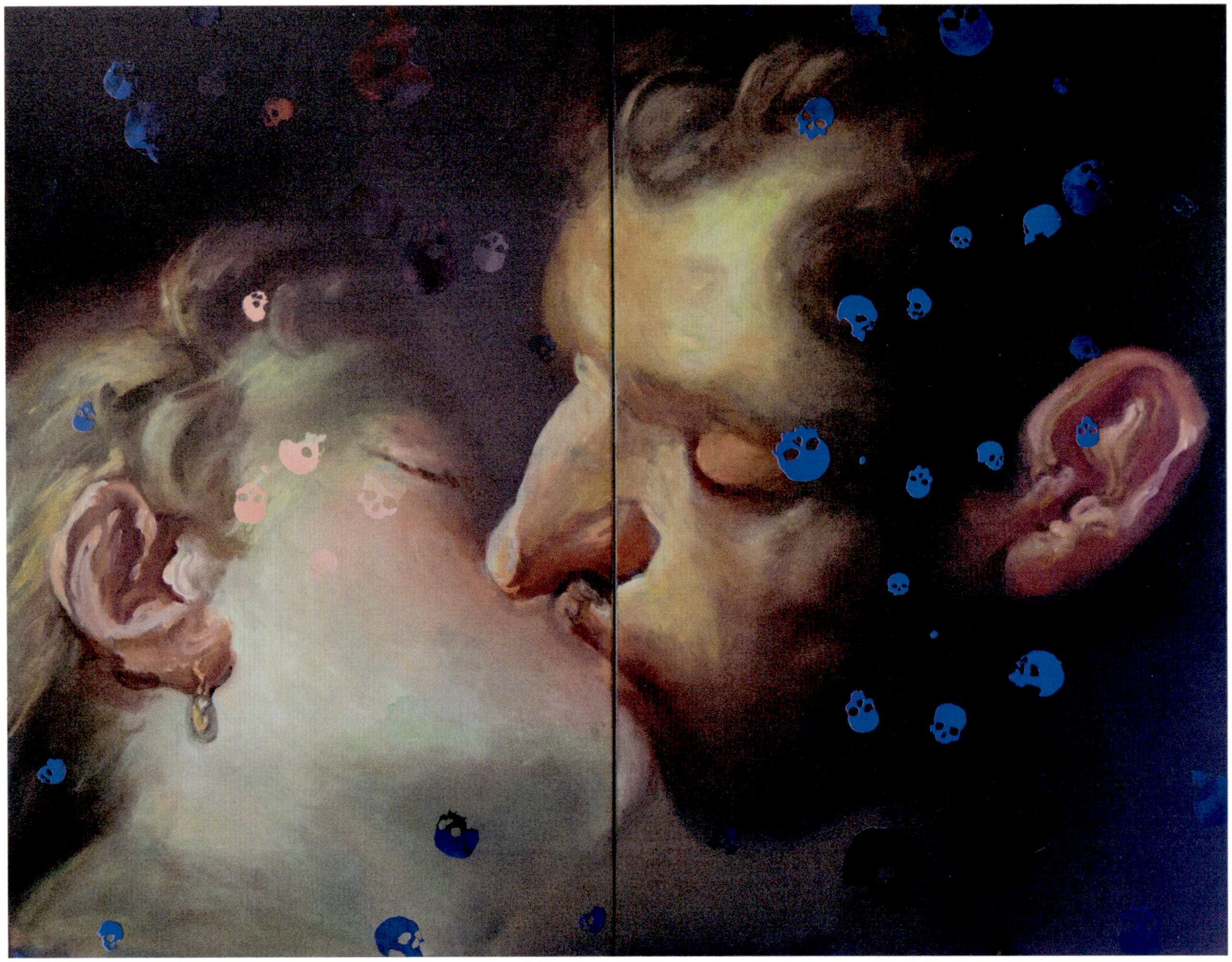

29

Kiss, 2017
Diptych
Acrylic and oil on canvas
Each: 72 7/16 × 46 1/16 in. (184 × 117 cm)
Overall: 72 7/16 × 92 1/8 in. (184 × 234 cm)
COLLECTION OF THE ARTIST

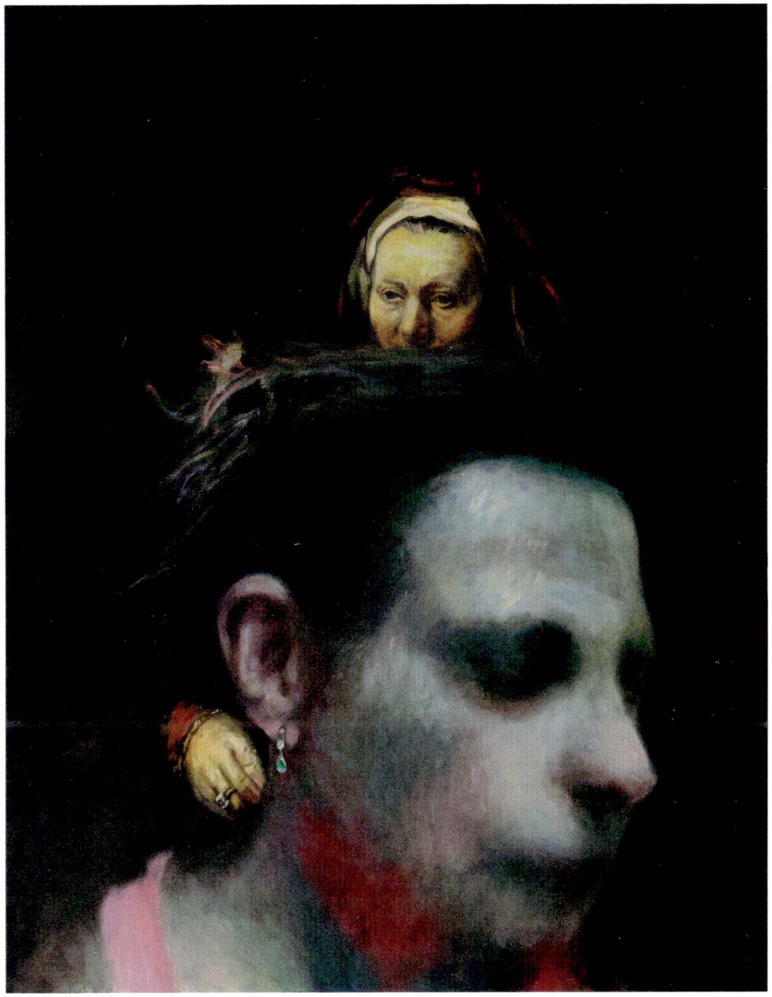

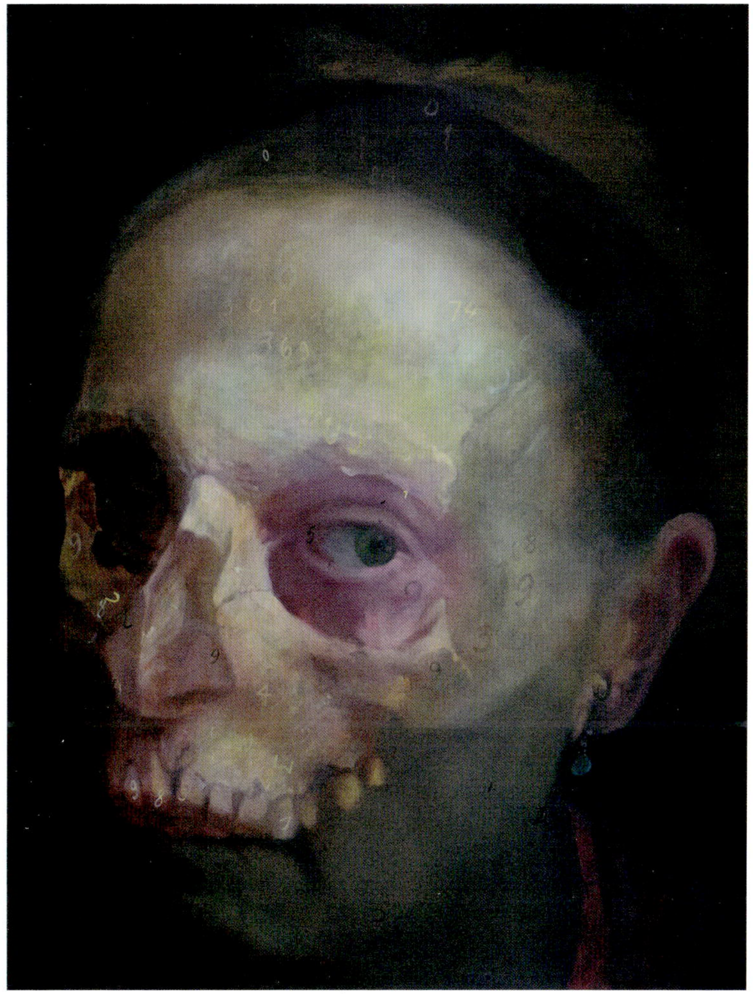

30

Vanitas 1 and 2, 2017

Acrylic and oil on canvas

Each: 78¾ × 59$\frac{1}{16}$ in. (200 × 150 cm)

COLLECTION OF THE ARTIST

IRINA NAKHOVA

Seven Masterpieces: An Audio Guide, 2013

The texts that follow are transcriptions in English of an audio guide created by Nakhova as part of an imaginary museum tour that was realized previously in 2013 at Moscow's Tretyakov Gallery, as part of the Contemporary Art Biennale, The Museum of Contemporary Art: Labor and Employment. *Viewers / museum visitors will hear these texts read as an audio guide as they walk through the Zimmerli galleries—missing are the artworks themselves. Only the labels (created by the artist as well) are available. Although some of the artists highlighted in this audio work are well-known historical figures in Russia, others are fictive. Nakhova has taken considerable liberty with the "facts" presented in each biography. Viewers/auditors must weigh their faith in the authority of the narrative against the possibility of deception, to recognize, as the artist explains, "the essence of didactic instruction."*

1 Ivan Aivazovsky

Ivan Kramskoi wrote, "Aivazovsky, whatever anyone might say, is a star of the first magnitude, and not just with us, but in the whole history of art."

Ivan Aivazovsky is one of only a few Russian artists who attained worldwide fame during his own lifetime. His self-portrait was hung in the Uffizi gallery in Florence. His widely acclaimed "wet dreams" (as his contemporaries called his superb seascapes) found their way all over the world.

Aivazovsky was a member of seventeen academies. He received many other honors and medals and was appointed chief artist of the Russian Navy. However, not many people know that he is also the most famous Armenian painter—he was of Armenian parentage, his original surname being Aivazian. Because his family was from Baku, he often visited that city and was known as Zizi by local friends and neighbors. Over time, he became very passionate about the development of the gas and oil industry in that region. In his paintings, he glorified the laborers on oil rigs and in the oil fields, while fulfilling commissions from local tycoons to paint murals in their palaces and mansions. He himself owned a few fields, but he never abandoned his work as an artist. He often said, "Who will do it, if not me?" The oil workers loved Zizi and often posed for him free of charge, as can be seen in this masterpiece, *The Depths*.

This work was saved for posterity only through the efforts of a certain Mrs. Karapetian, who in the difficult years of perestroika, hid the painting in her farm's pigsty, covered with manure. In 2005, after cleaning and restoration, Ms. Karapetian gave *The Depths* to the president, and thus saved a masterpiece from extinction.

The painting depicts the heroic labor on an oil rig, with the roaring sea about to engulf the brave workers. For sheer scale this work can only be compared to *The Ninth Wave*. The indigo and black palette speaks to us of never-ending natural resources and the great power of the Russian Empire, while reminding us of the careful use of this treasure, and it expresses both the fragility and the might of nature. If nature is not harnessed wisely, it can be ruthless to men in helmets. The crude oil is masterfully depicted. Aivazovsky employed the innovative technique of splashing oil on the surface of the painting, foreshadowing the work of Jackson Pollock by more than a half century.

2 Together Group

The work of the artist as researcher and designer is presented as a young creative couple in *Together*. This interactive installation combines a representation of the intellectual work of the artist and the physical work of a viewer. *Together* explores the past of our country based on the *Moscow Diary*, written in 1927 by Walter Benjamin, a philosopher and student of Russian cultural life.

During his first visit to the Kremlin, Benjamin was most fascinated by the abundance of different maps and diagrams. He wrote, "The geographical map is close to becoming a new icon for the Revolution, just as Lenin's portraits are." Benjamin describes an interactive map in the Red Army Club within the Kremlin: "A wooden relief map hangs on the wall; a schematically simplified outline of Europe. If you turn the handle next to it, all the places Lenin ever lived in Russia and Europe light up one after another in chronological sequence. But the apparatus works poorly; many places light up at the same time."

Together shifts the wooden wall relief into the horizontal plane and presents a map of Moscow made from matchboxes with built-in lights. There are also four heavy handles that turn only with great effort and quite a bit of squeaking. The map lights up, chronologically following Walter Benjamin's excursions around Moscow in December 1926 and January 1927, while also indicating all the buildings that Lenin visited. The contraption works intentionally poorly: when Benjamin's and Lenin's paths cross, short circuits occur and the matches that are still in a few of the boxes catch fire, as if igniting a revolutionary conflagration in Russia and Europe.

So the installation is primed to self-destruct with the help of the viewer. Water barriers around the matchbox relief symbolize the limited nature of Communist ideas and the stalwart defenses of the world's democracies. Social orientation, globalization, and political awareness are all components of this gentle yet radical installation in an urban setting. Environmental concern, an attractive, visually striking design, and knowledge of the subject reflect artistic tendencies of recent years, and this places *Together* alongside other, promising young, strong artistic pairings who are masters of their trade.

This installation has been made possible by the Moscow Water Board, the Moscow Electricity Board, Company "The Money Goes to the Bank," and the Moscow Match Factory.

3 Vasily Kandinsky

Vasily Kandinsky was the founder, theoretician, and trailblazer of abstract art, who opened up new horizons for visual creativity, liberating artists from copying their surroundings, and proclaiming a new expressiveness of color and feeling in free form.

Composition #3, which has the secondary title *Emancipated Labor*, has always been interpreted by scholars as the swan song of the artist's own emancipated labor.

In this masterpiece, Kandinsky asserts the priority of free movement and patches over flat colored planes, as if saying the artist's work lies in the free marking of the canvas with brushes no bigger than size 22. He rejects the use of flat brushes as inartistic, not worthy of any attention. From the chaos of small, boiling, fiery-red patches, blues disappearing saturatedly into the depth, and yellows aggressively moving towards the viewer, there emerges a forge, the quintessence of the artist's noble labor for the glory of future generations of abstract expressionists, who were freed by Kandinsky from unnecessary conceptual theorizing and directed by him straight into the abyss of free creativity.

These revolutionary ideas led Kandinsky to the idea of free enterprise. During the 1920s, he successfully created a network of artistic gymnastics clubs in Berlin. Those clubs provided him with a considerable income and gave him the opportunity to be a free artist. He invented and popularized a new form of floor routine called "Exercise with a Brush." This became the most popular form of gymnastics by late 1925, and not "Indian Club Drill," as certain scholars claim.

Kandinsky's work as an artist brought him only posthumous fame. During his lifetime, though, he inspired millions of amateurs and professionals to "exercise with a brush."

The phrase "I can do that too" is ascribed to Kandinsky's son from his third marriage. As a teenager, Theodore successfully created and sold copies of many paintings by his distinguished father.

4 Krutoi-Pliushchev

The twenty-first-century masterpiece *The Artist Entertains Potential Clients* by Misha Krutoi-Pliushchev reflects the theme of the artist's hard work to fulfill his social, tactical, and strategic goals during a time of primary accumulation of capital.

With warm humor, the artist confides to the viewer his anxiety for the future of art. In this interactive installation, Krutoi-Pliushchev uses ten automated vending machines to touch upon themes such as the artist and those in power, the artist and money, the unpredictability of the art market, and the ups and downs of the artist's existence in capitalist society.

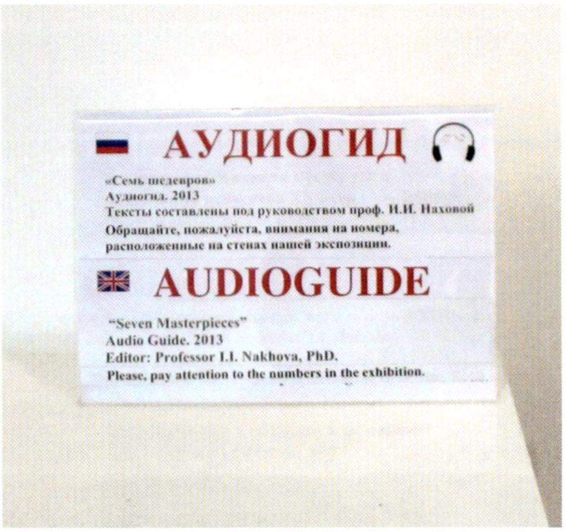

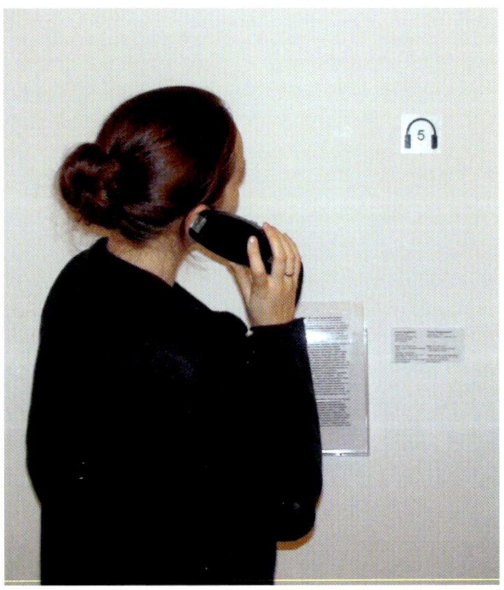

Seven Masterpieces: An Audio Guide, State Tretyakov Gallery, Moscow, 2013

The viewer puts 1,000 rubles into the machine and can get a glass of wine or a piece of art in return. Elements of chance, game playing, and a critique of gambling are brilliantly encapsulated in this work by the artist. The vending machine sculptures were cast in bronze at the famous Carrara workshops in southern Italy. The incomparable quality of material and sculptural form uses bronze to mimic cheap painted metal; the sculptures resemble early refrigerators from the 1950s or Soviet-era vending machines that dispensed aerated water infused with fruit syrup.

These sculptures place Krutoi-Pliushchev alongside outstanding nonconformist artists of the 1970s, who made superb use of found objects in their art to express criticism of the Soviet regime. This nostalgia for a time when artists were dependent more on the state than on direct financing reflects the artist's skepticism towards the contemporary art industry. Along with a glass of wine, he offers the viewer hope for the renaissance of humanistic art, aimed at ordinary folk, rather than a moneyed elite.

5 Ilya Repin

The traditional Russian work song, "Эй, ухнем!"—which roughly translates as "Yo, Heave-ho" but is known in English as the "Song of the Volga Boatmen"—inspired the great artist Ilya Repin to paint his famous work depicting *burlaki*, or barge haulers, on the great Russian river. The painting shows the suffering and unbearable toil of common people in tsarist Russia.

Burlakov was a wealthy Volga merchant who was just and honest. Simple peasants sought to join his particular teams of barge haulers, and that is why they became *burlaki*.

According to Repin's memoirs, the idea for the painting came to him in 1869, when he first saw the barge haulers while he was painting plein-air studies on the River Neva. He was struck by the enormous contrast between the merry society of city folk, relaxing at their dachas in the picturesque countryside near Saint Petersburg, and the pitiable lot of the barge haulers.

Repin's first studies consist of exhausted barge workers and typical holiday makers. The contrast was powerful, but labored. Ivan Kramskoi noticed this artificiality, and gave Repin (who was hard-pressed for money at the time) 200 rubles to travel to the Volga in order to study the customs and characteristics of the common people. In May 1870, the artist, with a small company of friends, set off by steamer.

Repin wrote in his memoirs entitled *So Far—So Close*: "What a horror it is—I say it straight—people are harnessed instead of animals! . . . Surely it is possible to transport a barge with a load in a decent manner, using tugboats, say. I have to honestly confess that I was not the least interested in the everyday life or social aspects of the barge haulers' contracts with their bosses; I only asked them to add some seriousness to the matter."

The artist was drawn mostly to typical Russians: "God, how marvelously that rag is tied around his head, how the hair is curling towards the neck . . . but most importantly—the color of his face."

In March of 1873, Repin finished his work. In the same year, *Burlaki on the Volga River* was shown in Vienna at the World's Fair and was purchased by Grand Duke Vladimir Alexandrovich for 3,000 rubles. He hung it on the wall in the billiards room of his grand palace. "I have to tell the truth," Repin wrote. "The Grand Duke sincerely liked the painting. He was fond of explaining some of the characters in the painting: the unfrocked priest Kanin, the soldier Zotov, the prizefighter from Nizhny Novgorod, and the impatient boy smarter than all of his older comrades. The Grand Duke was familiar with them all—I heard it with my own ears the keen interest with which he explained it all, down to the last hints in the background and landscape."

6 Vasily Tropinin

Vasily Tropinin was born into a family of serfs. Fortunately, his father, Prince Vysheslavisev, saw to it that he got a good education. From an early age Tropinin was drawn to the beauty of nature. It was said that as a boy, he wove exceptionally attractive floral wreaths that foreshadowed his future achievements.

In his work, Tropinin praises the discreet charm of serf labor: the locksmith, the stove maker, the barn guard, the dishwasher, and round dancers. In 1823, when he was already forty-three years old, the artist was unexpectedly freed by his owner, and he moved to Moscow. There, he painted his famous *The Lacemaker*, with nostalgia for rural village life. With unsurpassed attention to true-to-life detail, he became one of the founders of Russian realism. With a tiny brush, Tropinin depicts carefree, quiet provincial life with its modest occupations. In the painting, a sweet, playful lacemaker concentrates on her work; the bobbins are painted with great persuasiveness and look almost real. Simple-hearted and tender, and with a slight smile, the girl looks expectantly at the viewer, who could perhaps be her master, for whom she always waits.

Tropinin was at times accused of overt sentimentality, and to this he replied, "But I do not invent, I do not make up these smiles, I paint them from life. In real life, who wants to look at an angry, sullen face?" It is said that the artist portrayed his mother, Taisia, in *The Lacemaker*. The painting shines with a gentle love, tenderness in the gaze and in the colors.

In the sixties, during a time of developing counterculture and feminism, including the civil rights struggles of Blacks in the United States and Jews in the Soviet Union, *The Lacemaker* became a symbol of the fight for equal rights for gay, lesbian, bisexual, and transgender people. Even now, *The Lacemaker* makes officials responsible for law enforcement shudder at every arrest of anyone from the LGBT community. At any time, a teenager or young girl with plaits might pull out a copy of the painting from beneath a shabby jacket, to show solidarity with the victims of the Law.

7 Nikolai Yaroshenko

The oeuvre of Nikolai Yaroshenko was formed under the influence of the democratic ideas of the Russian Revolutionaries. Contemporaries called him the "Conscience of Itinerants."

The painter was born and raised in a family of peasant serfs. The boy's artistic talent became evident at a very young age. He copied banknotes with passion and precision; "You can't tell the difference," his folks would say.

Through this, Yaroshenko caught the attention of Leo Tolstoy, a local landowner. The count provided for the further education of the self-taught artist. Hard work in a group of local copyists bore fruit. In his major masterpiece of 1889, *The Insulted and Humiliated*, his accuracy of hand and keen vision are in full evidence. The dull grayish tone of this relatively small canvas pulls the viewer into the confined, suffocating environment of a secret counterfeiting shop. The men here are working against a State that never gave them anything but a debilitating sixteen-hour day. The bent backs and intense, blank stares seem to tell us that these men will soon straighten up, their gazes will clear, and, in the words of Gorky, "Soon the Storm will break!"

A lamp flaring in the upper right-hand corner of the painting also attests to the coming storm. Glowing red revolutionary flames are reflected in the workers' printing presses, blackened by grief and sorrow; they make the pile of bottles in the foreground sparkle, and flare up in the watery eyes of the elderly worker, the teenage apprentice, and the young worker bent over, intently studying their handiwork through a magnifying glass. "The Storm, soon the Storm will break!"

Yaroshenko's characters are painted with great sympathy and understanding; the three generations of workers are allegorical. "The Insulted and Humiliated" are the victims of the regime, of alcohol abuse, lack of education, and greed. The concrete and realistic visual language of Russian genre painting was directed to the understanding of the most oppressed classes. In 1927, Walter Benjamin wrote of the Tretyakov, "Walls full of narrative paintings, representations of scenes from all walks of life transform the gallery into a vast children's book."

Nearly a century later, this kind of artwork is still the most loved and appreciated by the public.

Works in the Exhibition

***Untitled*, 1978**
Four-part work
Oil on canvas
Each part: $13\frac{1}{16} \times 16\frac{1}{4}$ in. (33×41 cm)
Overall: $26\frac{3}{16} \times 32\frac{1}{2}$ in. (66.5×82.5 cm)
Norton and Nancy Dodge Collection of
Nonconformist Art from the Soviet Union
ZIMMERLI ART MUSEUM
D01148.01–04
PLATE 1

***Room No. 1*, 1983**
Gelatin silver print on paper
$11\frac{1}{8} \times 13\frac{7}{8}$ in. (28.2×35.3 cm)
Norton and Nancy Dodge Collection of
Nonconformist Art from the Soviet Union
ZIMMERLI ART MUSEUM
2000.1195
PLATE 2

***Room No. 1*, 1983**
Gelatin silver print on paper
$11\frac{1}{8} \times 13\frac{7}{8}$ in. (28.2×35.3 cm)
Norton and Nancy Dodge Collection of
Nonconformist Art from the Soviet Union
ZIMMERLI ART MUSEUM
2000.1196
PLATE 2

***Variable Landscape*, 1983**
Twenty-five panels
Oil on gessoed Masonite
Each: $9\frac{13}{16} \times 9\frac{13}{16}$ in. (25×25 cm)
Norton and Nancy Dodge Collection of
Nonconformist Art from the Soviet Union
ZIMMERLI ART MUSEUM
2013.016.064.01–25
PLATE 3

***Room No. 2*, 1984**
Gelatin silver print on paper
$11\frac{1}{16} \times 13\frac{15}{16}$ in. (28.1×35.4 cm)
Norton and Nancy Dodge Collection of
Nonconformist Art from the Soviet Union
ZIMMERLI ART MUSEUM
2000.1202
PLATE 4

***Room No. 2*, 1984**
Gelatin silver print on paper
$11 \times 13\frac{15}{16}$ in. (28.1×35.4 cm)
Norton and Nancy Dodge Collection of
Nonconformist Art from the Soviet Union
ZIMMERLI ART MUSEUM
2000.1203
PLATE 4

***Room No. 2*, 1984**
Gelatin silver print on paper
$11\frac{1}{8} \times 13\frac{5}{16}$ in. (28.2×35.4 cm)
Norton and Nancy Dodge Collection of
Nonconformist Art from the Soviet Union
ZIMMERLI ART MUSEUM
2000.1204
PLATE 4

***Room No. 2*, 1984**
Gelatin silver print on paper
$11\frac{1}{8} \times 13\frac{15}{16}$ in. (28.2×35.4 cm)
Norton and Nancy Dodge Collection of
Nonconformist Art from the Soviet Union
ZIMMERLI ART MUSEUM
2000.1205
PLATE 4

***Scaffolding*, 1984**
Diptych
Oil on canvas
Each: 59×59 in. (150×150 cm)
Norton and Nancy Dodge Collection of
Nonconformist Art from the Soviet Union
ZIMMERLI ART MUSEUM
D01148.01–02
PLATE 5

***Untitled*, 1985**
Collage, newspaper, gouache, and watercolor
$18\frac{15}{16} \times 14\frac{3}{16}$ in. (48×36 cm)
Norton and Nancy Dodge Collection of
Nonconformist Art from the Soviet Union
ZIMMERLI ART MUSEUM
D02084
PLATE 6

***Untitled*, 1985**
Collage, newspaper, gouache, and watercolor
$14\frac{3}{16} \times 18\frac{15}{16}$ in. (36×48 cm)
Norton and Nancy Dodge Collection of
Nonconformist Art from the Soviet Union
ZIMMERLI ART MUSEUM
D04652
PLATE 6

***Untitled*, 1985**
Collage, newspaper, gouache, and watercolor
$18\frac{15}{16} \times 14\frac{3}{16}$ in. (48×36 cm)
Norton and Nancy Dodge Collection of
Nonconformist Art from the Soviet Union
ZIMMERLI ART MUSEUM
D04653
PLATE 6

Untitled, 1985
Collage, newspaper, gouache, and watercolor
$14\frac{3}{16} \times 18\frac{15}{16}$ in. (36 × 48 cm)
Norton and Nancy Dodge Collection of
Nonconformist Art from the Soviet Union
ZIMMERLI ART MUSEUM
D04654
PLATE 6

Untitled, 1985
Collage, newspaper, and watercolor
$18\frac{15}{16} \times 14\frac{3}{16}$ in. (48 × 36 cm)
Norton and Nancy Dodge Collection of
Nonconformist Art from the Soviet Union
ZIMMERLI ART MUSEUM
D20469
PLATE 6

Room No. 4, 1986
Gelatin silver print on paper
11⅛ × 13⅞ in. (28.2 × 35.3 cm)
Norton and Nancy Dodge Collection of
Nonconformist Art from the Soviet Union
ZIMMERLI ART MUSEUM
2000.1197
PLATE 7

Room No. 4, 1985
Gelatin silver print on paper
11⅛ × 13⅞ in. (28.2 × 35.3 cm)
Norton and Nancy Dodge Collection of
Nonconformist Art from the Soviet Union
ZIMMERLI ART MUSEUM
2000.1198
PLATE 7

Double Vision, 1988
Polyptych, two of four panels
Acrylic and oil on canvas
Each: 59 × 78¾ in. (150 × 200 cm)
COLLECTION OF THE ARTIST
PLATE 8

Camping, 1990
Acrylic and oil on canvas, army cots
Each: 78 × 28½ × 15 in. (198 × 72 × 38 cm)
Four pieces from the series:
Three: COLLECTION OF THE ARTIST
One: Gift of Vals Osborne and
José Moreno-Lacalle
ZIMMERLI ART MUSEUM
2017.011.010
PLATE 9

Mobeus, 1990
Diptych
Acrylic and oil on shaped canvas
Overall: 49 × 156 in. (124 × 396 cm)
COLLECTION OF THE ARTIST
PLATE 10

Momentum Mortis, 1990
Two panels from the original installation
at Phyllis Kind Gallery
Polyurethane foam, dirt, sand, and
acrylic on canvas
84 × 60 × 5 in. (214 × 152 × 12 cm)
84 × 60 × 5 in. (214 × 152 × 12 cm)
Norton and Nancy Dodge Collection of
Nonconformist Art from the Soviet Union
ZIMMERLI ART MUSEUM
PLATE 11

Untitled, 1990
Watercolor, gouache, and crayon on paper
14⅛ × 19⅝ in. (36 × 50 cm)
Gift of Vals Osborne and José Moreno-Lacalle
ZIMMERLI ART MUSEUM
2017.011.011
PLATE 12

Untitled, 1990
Watercolor and crayon on paper
13¾ × 16⅞ in. (35 × 43 cm)
Gift of Vals Osborne and José Moreno-Lacalle
ZIMMERLI ART MUSEUM
2017.011.012
PLATE 13

Eye, 1992
Oil, acrylic, and plaster on Masonite
Panel (irregular): 31⅜ × 45¼ × 1 in.
(79.7 × 115 × 2.5 cm)
Gift of Vals Osborne and José Moreno-Lacalle
ZIMMERLI ART MUSEUM
2017.011.013
PLATE 14

***Four Torsos* from the *Untitled* installation at Phyllis Kind Gallery**, 1992
Plaster and mixed media
20 × 19½ × 5½ in. (51 × 50 × 14 cm)
20½ × 16½ × 5 in. (52 × 42 × 13 cm)
27½ × 19½ × 4 in. (70 × 50 × 10 cm)
24½ × 22 × 5 in. (62 × 56 × 13 cm)
COLLECTION OF THE ARTIST
PLATE 15

Queen (Video), 1996
Video, 25:29 mins.
COLLECTION OF THE ARTIST
PLATE 16

Queen, 1996
Iron, aluminum, papier-mâché,
parachute silk, and wooden pedestal with
electrical and electronic parts
93½ × 27 × 27 in. (238 × 69 × 69 cm) deflated
144 × 27 × 27 in. (366 × 69 × 69 cm) inflated
COLLECTION OF THE ARTIST
PLATE 17

Annunciation: Red Angels, 2000
Three inflatable angels from a
series of twelve
Parachute silk inflatables, electronics, fans
19 × 38 × 24 in. (48 × 97 × 61 cm) inflated
17 × 42 × 23 in. (43 × 107 × 58 cm) inflated
19 × 51 × 30 (48 × 130 × 76 cm) inflated
COLLECTION OF THE ARTIST
PLATE 18

Skin No. 1, 2010
Inkjet print on latex
30½ × 21½ in. (77 × 54 cm)
COLLECTION OF THE ARTIST
PLATE 19

Skin No. 3, 2010
Inkjet print on latex
33 × 28 in. (85 × 69 cm)
COLLECTION OF THE ARTIST
PLATE 20

Skin No. 4, 2010
Inkjet print on latex
22 × 24½ in. (55 × 62 cm)
COLLECTION OF THE ARTIST
PLATE 21

Skin No. 5, 2010
Inkjet print on latex
35 × 25 in. (89 × 64 cm)
COLLECTION OF THE ARTIST
PLATE 22

Skin No. 10, 2010
Inkjet print on latex
27½ × 26 in. (71 × 66 cm)
COLLECTION OF THE ARTIST
PLATE 23

Seven Masterpieces: An Audio Guide, 2013
Seven audio recordings:
Aivazovsky, 2:47 mins.
Together Group, 2:52 mins.
Kandinsky, 2:25 mins.
Krutoi-Pliushchev, 2:03 mins.
Repin, 3:11 mins.
Tropinin, 2:31 mins.
Yaroshenko, 2:42 mins.
COLLECTION OF THE ARTIST

Gaze, 2016–19
Three videos based on works from the Pushkin
State Museum of Fine Arts, Moscow, all 2016:
Rembrandt, *Portrait of an Old Woman*,
1650–55. 8:00 mins
François Boucher, *Hercules and Omphale*,
1732–34. 7:41 mins.
Jean-Baptiste-Siméon Chardin, *Still Life with Attributes of the Arts*, c. 1724–28. 3:34 mins.
One work based on a painting from the
Zimmerli Art Museum, Rutgers University, 2019:
Unidentified French artist, *Portrait of an Artist in Her Studio*, c. 1790. 7:06 mins.
COLLECTION OF THE ARTIST
PLATE 24–27

Battle of the Invalids, 2017
Installation: Papier-mâché, UltraBoard,
radio-controlled cars
Video projection, 28:35 mins.
Ten sculptures, each 27 × 16 × 16 in. (69 × 40 × 40 cm)
COLLECTION OF THE ARTIST
PLATE 28

Kiss, 2017
Diptych
Acrylic and oil on canvas
Each: $72\frac{7}{16} \times 46\frac{1}{16}$ in. (184 × 117 cm)
Overall: $72\frac{7}{16}$ × 92⅛ in. (184 × 234 cm)
COLLECTION OF THE ARTIST
PLATE 29

Vanitas 1, 2017
Acrylic and oil on canvas
78¾ × $59\frac{1}{16}$ in. (200 × 150 cm)
COLLECTION OF THE ARTIST
PLATE 30

Vanitas 2, 2017
Acrylic and oil on canvas
78¾ × $59\frac{1}{16}$ in. (200 × 150 cm)
COLLECTION OF THE ARTIST
PLATE 30

Selected Exhibitions

Asterisks indicate exhibitions with accompanying catalogues

Solo Exhibitions

2017

Battle of the Invalids, pop/off/art gallery, Moscow

2016

Gaze, Pushkin State Museum of Fine Arts, Moscow

Irina Nakhova: Presence, Nailya Alexander Gallery, New York

2015

The Green Pavilion. Representing Russia at the 56th International Art Exhibition, Venice Biennale*

2014

Irina Nakhova: Moscow Diary, Nailya Alexander Gallery, New York

Paradise, Winzavod Center for Contemporary Art, Moscow

2012

Renovation, Stella Art Foundation, Moscow

2011

Strange Primer, ERA Foundation, Moscow

Rooms, Moscow Museum of Modern Art*

2010

Irina Nakhova and Pavel Pepperstein: Moscow Partisan Conceptualism, Orel Art UK, London*

2009

Disconnected, Open Gallery, Moscow*

2008

Zone of No Distinction, XL Gallery, Moscow

2007

Disagreeable Matters—Disarming Icons, Windows, Kimmel Galleries, New York University

2006

Trip, XL Gallery, Moscow*

Moscow Installation, BBK Karlsruhe

2005

Artificial Shrubbery, State Tretyakov Gallery, Moscow

Probably Would, Nailya Alexander Gallery, New York

Two New, Kresge Gallery, Ramapo College, Mahwah, New Jersey

2004

Alert: Code Orange, National Centre for Contemporary Arts, Moscow

Us, XL Gallery, Moscow

Silence, Galerie im Traklhaus, Salzburg*

2003

When Will You Be Home?, College of Wooster Art Museum, Ohio

Rehearsal, State Tretyakov Gallery, Moscow

2002

Stay With Me, XL Gallery, Moscow*

2001

Annunciation, XL Gallery, Moscow*

2000

Deposition, Rupertinum, Museum der Moderne, Salzburg

1999

Big Red, XL Gallery, Moscow*

Archeology of the Room, Gallery Obscuri Viri, Moscow

1998

Showroom: Installation with Big Red, Galerie Eboran, Salzburg. Traveled to Tallinn City Gallery

Honeybuns Performing Goethe's Werther, with Günter Unterburger, Galerie im Alcatraz, Hallein, Austria*

1997

What I Saw, XL Gallery, Moscow*

Power of Painting: Food Painting, Bunting Gallery, Royal Oak, Michigan

1996

Daddy Needs to Relax, Gallery Obscuri Viri, Moscow*

1995

Friends and Neighbors, Cranbrook Art Museum, Bloomfield Hills, Michigan

Feast for the Gods, XL Gallery, Moscow*

1993

Careful with Your Eyes, Gallery 60, Bildmuseet, Umeå, Sweden

1992

In Memoriam, Chicago International Art Exposition, Special Project Installation

Recent Works, Phyllis Kind Gallery, New York

1991

Partial Triumph II, Galeria Berini, Barcelona

1990

Momentum Mortis, Phyllis Kind Gallery, New York

1989

Partial Triumph I, Vanessa Devereux Gallery, London*

Selected Group Exhibitions

2018

Performer and Participant, Tate Modern, London

Numbers and Digits, Museum Centre, Russian State University for the Humanities, Moscow*

2017

HYBRIS, Ca' Foscari, Venice*

Innovation Prize: 2017, Shchusev State Museum of Architecture, Moscow*

Red Horizon: Contemporary Art and Photography in the USSR and Russia, 1960–2010, Columbus Art Museum, Ohio*

A Vibrant Field: Nature and Landscape in Soviet Nonconformist Art, Zimmerli Art Museum, New Brunswick, New Jersey

Cyland Media Art Laboratory 10 Years, Scientific-Research Museum of the Academy of Arts of Russia, Saint Petersburg*

2016

Russian Artists: Participants of the Venice Biennale, Central Exhibition Hall Manege, Moscow*

"Thinking Pictures": Moscow Conceptual Art in the Dodge Collection, Zimmerli Art Museum, Rutgers University, New Brunswick, New Jersey*

House of Impression: Classic and Contemporary Media Art, Pushkin State Museum of Fine Arts, Moscow*

Primary Forces, Nailya Alexander Gallery, New York

The Modern Art: 1960–2000. Restart, State Tretyakov Gallery, Moscow

2015

Contemporaries of the Future: Jewish Artists in the Russian Avant-Garde, Jewish Museum and Tolerance Center, Moscow*

Urbi et Orbi, Museum Centre, Russian State University for the Humanities, Moscow*

2014

Post Pop: East Meets West, Saatchi Gallery, London*

2013

Migrants, Museum Centre, Russian State University for the Humanities, Moscow*

Wolves and Sheep, State Literary Museum, Moscow*

Museum of Contemporary Art: Department of Labor and Employment, State Tretyakov Gallery, Moscow*

Kandinsky Prize Finalists, Moscow*

International Women's Day. Feminism: From Avant-Garde to the Present Day, Manege, Worker and Kolkhoz Woman Center, Moscow*

2012

Decoration of the Beautiful, Elitism and Kitsch in Contemporary Art, State Tretyakov Gallery, Moscow*

John Cage: Silent Presence, National Centre for Contemporary Arts, Moscow*

2011

Hostages of Void: Aesthetics of Empty Space in Russian Art During the 19th–20th Centuries, State Tretyakov Gallery, Moscow*

2010

Visual/Conceptual, National Centre for Contemporary Arts, Moscow*

Doors Open Day: a mansion—a gymnasium—a clinic—a museum. Russian Art, 1989–2009, from the Collection of the Moscow Museum of Modern Art, Moscow Museum of Modern Art*

Horror, E. K. ArtBureau, Moscow

Shelter, E. K. ArtBureau, Moscow

Field of Action, Moscow Conceptual School and Its Context, 70s and 80s of the 20th Century, Ekaterina Cultural Foundation, Moscow*

2009

History of Russian Video Art, Volume 2, Moscow Museum of Modern Art*

The Secret Life of Bodies, Open Gallery, Moscow*

Russian Lettrism, Central House of Artists, Moscow

Not Toys!?, State Tretyakov Gallery, Moscow*

Vulnerability, Museum Center, Russian State University for the Humanities, Moscow*

Dead Souls, State Literary Museum, Moscow*

2008

+7 (495) . . . Russian Artists Abroad: Works from NCCA Collection, National Centre for Contemporary Arts, Moscow*

Kandinsky Prize, Exhibition of Selected Nominees, Riga; Palazzo Italia, Milan; and Berlin*

2007

This Is Not Food, ERA Foundation, Moscow*

Kandinsky Prize, Exhibition of the Nominees, Winzavod Centre for Contemporary Art, Moscow*

New in the Collection, National Centre for Contemporary Arts, Moscow*

History of Russian Video Art, Volume 1, Moscow Museum of Contemporary Art*

I Believe!, Winzavod Centre for Contemporary Art, Moscow*

Katoptron (Direction of a Mirror Glance), Museum Centre, Russian State University for the Humanities, Moscow*

Nostalgia, Neal Davis Gallery, Royal Oak, Michigan

Apocalypse: Contemporary Visions, Candace Dwan and Nailya Alexander Galleries, New York

2006

Territories of Terror: Mythologies and Memories of the Gulag in Contemporary Russian-American Art, Boston University Art Gallery*

Artists Against the State: Perestroika Revisited, Ronald Feldman Gallery, New York

Collage in Russia: 20th Century, State Russian Museum, Saint Petersburg*

Homo Grandis Natu: Age, Museum Centre, Russian State University for the Humanities, Moscow

2005

Reflection, National Centre for Contemporary Arts, Moscow*

Gender Troubles, Moscow Museum of Contemporary Art*

Accomplices: Collective and Interactive Works in Russian Art of the 1960s–2000, State Tretyakov Gallery, Moscow*

Egalitarianism, Museum Centre, Russian State University for the Humanities, Moscow*

Apartment Exhibitions: Yesterday and Today, National Centre for Contemporary Arts, Moscow

Allusive Form: Painting as Idea, Zimmerli Art Museum, Rutgers University, New Brunswick, New Jersey

2004

Beyond Memory, Zimmerli Art Museum, Rutgers University, New Brunswick, New Jersey*

Body, Culture and Optical Illusions, Museum Centre, Russian State University for the Humanities, Moscow*

2003

Luleå Biennial, Kilen, The Artists Group in Luleå, Sweden*

Berlin–Moscow / Moscow–Berlin, 1950–2000, Martin-Gropius-Bau, Berlin; State Tretyakov Gallery, Moscow*

3rd International Biennial of Contemporary Graphics 2003, State Art Museum, Novosibirsk, Russia*

Tests of Time: Five Reflections, Jewish Community Center, Manhattan, New York

Contemporary Art Celebrating Life, Allegheny Cemetery, Pittsburgh

2002

Iskusstvo zhenskogo roda, State Tretyakov Gallery, Moscow*

Aquaria, Oberösterreichisches Landesmuseum, Linz, Austria; Kunstsammlungen Chemnitz, Germany*

mind/body, Bristol-Myers Squibb Gallery, Princeton*

Moscow Time, Contemporary Art Centre, Vilnius; National Centre for Contemporary Arts, Nizhny Novgorod*

2001

Milano Europa 2000, Padiglione d'Arte Contemporanea, Milan*

Dumbo Double Deuce, Russian American Cultural Center, 10 Jay Street, DUMBO, Brooklyn

Women Artists from the Dodge Collection, Zimmerli Art Museum, Rutgers University, New Brunswick, New Jersey

Four Women and Their Ironing Boards, Artemisia Gallery, Chicago

2000

Seeing Isn't Believing: Russian Art Since Glasnost, Lamont Gallery, Phillips Exeter Academy, Exeter, New Hampshire*

Russian Artists of the 1960s–1990s, Schimmel Center at Pace University, New York

Polar Cold: Inspection Medical Hermeneutics and Russian Art of the '90s, Krasnoyarsk, Russia. Traveled to École Nationale Supérieure des Beaux-Arts, Paris

LandEscape, Dieu Donné Papermill, New York

1999

International Forum of Art Initiatives, State Exhibition Hall, Maly Manege, Moscow

Global Conceptualism: Points of Origin, 1950s–1980s, Queens Museum, New York*

My First Work, Galleries at Pasadena City College, California*

Collector's Edge, Visual Arts Center of New Jersey, Summit

Russia Without a Museum of Contemporary Art, Part 2, XL Gallery, Leverkusen, Germany

Contemporary Art from 1950s to 1980s from Tsaritsyno Museum Collection, Central House of Artists, Moscow

Fauna, National Centre for Contemporary Arts, State Exhibition Hall, Maly Manege, Moscow

Women in Art, Kolodzei Art Foundation, Chevy Chase, Maryland. Traveled to Russian Consulate and Friendship Gallery, New York

Sculpture—Figure—Woman, Oberösterreichisches Landesmuseum, Linz, Austria. Traveled to Kunstsammlungen Chemnitz, Germany*

Präprintium, Staatsbibliothek Berlin. Traveled to Neues Museum Weserburg, Bremen*

Art Forum Berlin, Berlin (with XL Gallery)

Modernism and Post-Modernism: Russian Art of the Ending Millennium, Yager Museum of Art & Culture, Hartwick College, Oneonta, New York* (traveling exhibition)

Self-Portrait, Dieu Donné Papermill, New York

1997

Russian Art in Fifteen Destinies, Mucsarnok, State Exhibition Hall, Budapest

RUM, Edsvik Konsthall och Kultur, Stockholm

Margareta x 4, Kalmar Konstmuseum, Sweden*

Square Meal, Community Art Gallery, Wayne State University, Detroit (organizer and participant)

Abandoned Building Investigation, Pontiac Building, Wayne State University, Detroit (organizer and participant)

Moscow International Art Fair, State Exhibition Hall, Maly Manege, Moscow

1996

How to Draw a Horse, Central House of Artists, Moscow

Wayne State University Art Faculty Exhibition, Community Arts Gallery, Detroit

Pulp Fusion, 5501 Columbia Art Center, Dallas

Time Is Now, Detroit Focus Gallery

Family Values: Rhetoric vs. Reality, T. W. Wood Gallery, Montpelier, Vermont

International Forum of Art Initiatives, State Exhibition Hall, Maly Manege, Moscow

1995

City Limits, Paint Creek Center for the Arts, Rochester, Michigan

Fellowship Recipients, Rutgers Center for Innovative Printmaking, Mason Gross School of the Arts, Rutgers University, Piscataway, New Jersey

Cathedral of Time: A Collaborative Installation Organized by Irina Nakhova, Michigan Central Depot, Detroit*

Non-Conformists in Russia, 1957–1985: Wilhelm-Hack-Museum, Ludwigshafen, Germany. Traveled to Documenta Halle, Kassel, Germany; Lindenau-Museum, Altenburg, Germany; Central Exhibition Hall, Manege, Moscow*

5 + 5, Educational Alliance, New York City

From Gulag to Glasnost: Nonconformist Art from the Soviet Union, The Norton and Nancy Dodge Collection, Zimmerli Art Museum, Rutgers University, New Brunswick, New Jersey*

The Holiday Show: Objects for and about the Holidays, Center Galleries, Detroit

Dieu Donné Editions, 1988–1995, Dieu Donné Papermill, New York

Silent Auction Exhibition, Dieu Donné Papermill, New York

Laughter Ten Years After. Traveled to six museums and galleries, United States and Canada*

Wayne State University Art Faculty Exhibition, Community Arts Gallery, Detroit

1994

Fellowship Recipients, Rutgers Center for Innovative Printmaking, Mason Gross School of the Arts, Rutgers University, Piscataway, New Jersey

Natural Histories, Pyramid Atlantic Art Center, Riverdale, Maryland

Paper, Process, Art, Art Gallery, Suffolk Community College, Selden, New York

Artist Instead of an Art Work, Central House of Artists, Moscow

Dialogue with the Other, Kunsthallen Brandts Klaedefabrik, Odense, Denmark. Traveled to Norrköping Konstmuseum, Sweden*

Cetinje Biennial, Cetinje Art Museum, Serbia*

Before "Neo" and After "Post," Lehman College Art Gallery, New York*

Impressions of Lakeside, Bunting Gallery, Royal Oak, Michigan

Monumental Propaganda, International Gallery, Smithsonian Institution, Washington, DC*

1993

Adresse Provisoire, Musée de la Poste, Paris*

Baltic Sculpture 93, Gotland Art Museum, Visby, Sweden*

After Perestroika: Kitchenmaids or Stateswomen, Independent Curators Incorporated (ICI). Traveled to six museums, United States and Canada*

Monumental Propaganda, traveling exhibition in USA and Russia*

Exchange, Granary Books, Susan Teller Gallery, New York

Careful with Your Eyes, Gallery 60, Konsthögskolan, Umeå, Sweden, and Sundsvalls Museum, Sweden

1992

Installations, Tsaritsyno Museum, Bratislava*

Group Exhibition, Lakeside Gallery, Lakeside, Michigan

A Mosca . . . a Mosca . . ., Villa Campolieto, Herculaneum, Italy; Galleria Bologna Museum of Modern Art*

A Changeable Feast: International Flavors, Walters Hall Gallery, Center for Innovative Printmaking, Rutgers University, New Brunswick, New Jersey

Master Prints, Bristol-Meyers Squibb Gallery, Princeton

Group Exhibition, Phyllis Kind Gallery, Chicago

1991

Passions on Strastnoj, First Gallery, Moscow

Moscow Avant-Garde Art, MANI Museum, Frankfurt*

Novecento, Central House of Artists, Moscow*

1990

Sommer Atelier, Messegelände Hannover, Germany*

Catalogue, Palace of Youth, Moscow*

Working Woman, Oktjabrskaja Exhibition Hall, Moscow

The Work of Art in the Age of Perestroika, Phyllis Kind Gallery, New York*

Iskonstvo: Stockholm-Moscow-Berlin, Kulturhuset, Stockholm*

Inexpensive Art, First Gallery, Moscow

The Storm Collection, Century Gallery, London*

1989

The Green Show, Exit Art, New York City*

Iskunstvo: Moscow-Berlin, Frunzenskaya Exhibition Hall, Moscow*

Expensive Art, Palace of Youth, Moscow

1988

USSR: New Tendencies, Arte Fiera, Bologna*

Ich lebe—Ich sehe, Kunstmuseum, Bern*

Iskunstvo: Moscow-Berlin, Bahnhof Berlin-Westend, West Berlin

Russian Avant-Garde and Soviet Contemporary Art, Sotheby's and USSR Ministry of Culture, exhibition and auction, International Trade Centre, Moscow*

Second Exhibition of the Avant-Gardists Club, Proletarsky District Exhibition Hall, Moscow

Neuvostoliiton Nuorta Taidetta, Turun Taidemuseo, Turku, Finland*

1987

The Artist and Modernism, Krasnogvardeisky District Exhibition Hall, Moscow

Representation, Hermitage Association, Moscow

Retrospection, 1957–1987, Hermitage Association, Exhibition Hall on Profsoyuznaya Street, Moscow

First Exhibition of Avant-Gardists Club, Proletarsky District Exhibition Hall, Moscow

1986

XVII Exhibition of Young Moscow Artists, Moscow House of Artists, Moscow

1985

All-Union Young Artists Exhibition, XII World Youth Student Festival, Moscow and other cities of the USSR

1984

XV Exhibition of Young Moscow Artists, Central Exhibition Hall, Manege, Moscow

Acknowledgments

Ambitious projects such as this exhibition and catalogue are made possible through the vision and generous funding provided by Norton and Nancy Dodge's legacy gift to Rutgers University, as well as by the Avenir Foundation, whose devotion to gaining recognition for the creative work by nonconformist visual artists from the Soviet Union remains a constant source of inspiration to us all. This exhibition and catalogue could be realized only through the close collaboration and professional expertise of all members of the Zimmerli staff, particularly Leslie Kriff, registrar; Kiki Michael, associate registrar; Stacy Smith, manager of publications and communications; Whitney Prendergast, director of development; and the indefatigable preparations team led by Keith Bull. We are grateful to Julia Tulovsky, curator of Russian and Soviet nonconformist art at the Zimmerli, and to Jane A. Sharp, research curator of the Dodge Collection of Nonconformist Art from the Soviet Union at the Zimmerli and professor in the Department of Art History at Rutgers. They organized the exhibition and served as general editors of the catalogue, with the assistance of two Rutgers art history department graduate students: Dodge Avenir Fellow Maria Garth and Dodge Lawrence Fellow Sopio Gagoshidze. Gabriella A. Ferrari, a Princeton University graduate student, assisted in identifying works for the exhibition and also made invaluable contributions to the catalogue. Natalia Sidlina, curator at Tate Modern, provided an insightful essay. We are deeply grateful to Irina Nakhova, for her participation and for lending works from her collection. We also extend our thanks to those who worked directly with Ms. Nakhova, especially Gordon Meldrum and Sergei Sinitsyn, and to John Tormey, in recognition of the effort and commitment required in bringing the work of this artist to light here at Rutgers University.

Thomas Sokolowski

Contributors

Gabriella A. Ferrari

is a PhD candidate at Princeton University in the Department of Slavic Languages and Literatures. She holds a BA in classics and Slavic studies from Brown University. Ferrari has previously worked as a Russian art cataloguer and researcher for Christie's Russian Art Department and Shapero Rare Books Gallery, both in London. Her current research focuses on modernist aesthetics, avant-garde theory, and the intersection of image, text, and materiality in Soviet culture. Her dissertation project investigates the role of propaganda objects in shaping the Soviet ideological landscape.

Jane A. Sharp

is professor in the Department of Art History at Rutgers University and research curator of the Dodge Collection of Nonconformist Art from the Soviet Union at the Zimmerli Art Museum. She has published widely on Soviet-era nonconformist art and on the historical Russian avant-garde, including an award-winning monograph, *Russian Modernism between East and West: Natalia Goncharova and the Moscow Avant-Garde* (Cambridge University Press, 2006). Her many exhibitions drawn from the Dodge Collection at the Zimmerli include *"Thinking Pictures": Moscow Conceptual Art in the Dodge Collection* (September 2016–January 2017). She is currently preparing a book manuscript on abstract painting in Moscow during and after the Thaw.

Natalia Sidlina

is curator of international art at Tate Modern, London. She has a BA in museum studies (State University of Humanities, Moscow), an MA in contemporary art history (Sorbonne University, Paris), and a PhD in art history (State Institute of Art Research, Moscow). She specializes in Russian émigré art and from 2005 has worked in Russian and British museums. Her recent exhibition projects include *Cosmonauts: Birth of the Space Age* at the Science Museum, London, in 2015, and *Eric Bulatov: Forward* and *Red Star Over Russia: A Revolution in Visual Culture, 1905–55*, both held at Tate Modern in 2017. She has also worked on archival research projects at the Gabo collection at Tate Archive for her monograph *Naum Gabo* (Tate Publishing, 2012) and at David King's private collection for the publication *Russian Revolutionary Posters* (Tate Publishing, 2012).

Julia Tulovsky

is curator of Russian and Soviet nonconformist art at the Zimmerli Art Museum at Rutgers University. She holds a PhD from Moscow State University, and her research focuses on the interconnections between the Russian and European avant-gardes of the 1920s, as well as on Soviet nonconformist and Russian contemporary art. Before coming to the Zimmerli, she was assistant curator at the State Tretyakov Gallery in Moscow and served as executive director of the Malevich Society in New York, currently remaining a member of its board. She has published widely on Russian art (avant-garde and contemporary), both in Russian and in English. Her most recent book is *Avant-Garde of the 1920s: Textile Designs* (Yekaterinburg: Tatlin, 2016).